Thyme to ENTERTAIN

GOOD FOOD AND SOUTHERN HOSPITALITY

CHARITY LEAGUE OF PADUCAH, KENTUCKY

Thank you for purchasing a copy of the first printing of
Thyme to Entertain, November, 2000

The Charity League, Inc.
of Paducah, Kentucky

is a non-profit, volunteer organization, whose mission includes raising funds for the Easter Seals West Kentucky and assisting other local non-profit organizations for the health, welfare and general care of children, women, and others in need. Our foremost purpose is in financially assisting Easter Seals West Kentucky and other charities, while secondarily creating a legacy of friendship and community with whom we work.

Changes that make life more satisfying do not occur overnight. Easter Seals West Kentucky helps create solutions for persons with disabilities to change their lives toward greater independence. The programs at Easter Seals West Kentucky are geared to developing the full potential of every person—morally, physically, cognitively, emotionally, educationally, socially, and vocationally. Easter Seals West Kentucky is a not-for-profit health agency established in 1954 by The Charity League, Inc. of Paducah, Kentucky and the Paducah Lions Club to assist children and adults with disabilities.

Additional copies of *Thyme to Entertain* may be obtained by sending
$20.95 plus $3.50 shipping to (KY residents add 6% sales tax):

The Charity League, Inc.
1921 Broadway
P.O. Box 7123
Paducah, Kentucky 42001

First Printing   November 2000   5,000 Copies

ISBN: 0-9701982-0-5

Library of Congress Number: 00-103505

Printed in the USA by

WIMMER
The Wimmer Companies
Memphis
1-800-548-2537

Thyme to Entertain

GOOD FOOD AND SOUTHERN HOSPITALITY

Smiles brighter than cake candles. Sweet scents swelling from mother's baking rack. Long embraces from long lost friends. Warm and buttery bread rising. Loud and laudatory toasts and salutations. Fiery flavors filling the grill. All of these wonderful moments and memories happen when we take "Thyme to Entertain". Whether it's hosting a black-tie gala honoring a granddaughter's engagement, winning over clients after hours at your home, or a spur of the moment celebration with special friends, entertaining is a part of our lives and plays an historical part of our community.

Paducah, Kentucky — nestled on the banks of the Ohio River in the heart of America. A community steeped in tradition, flavored by a rich history, and heralded for hospitality, we are proud to call Paducah our home. We take pride in Paducah's nationally known events and festivals. We enjoy the time we have with our families and friends, and we take the time to make our local events unique and memorable and our ordinary gatherings extra special. Paducah truly is a way of life.

In this cookbook, we have combined a sampling of Paducah's celebrations, history, and favorite ways to entertain with dazzling and savory menu selections for year round party giving. From simple southern dishes that comfort the most restless souls to contemporary cuisine that will tantalize and tingle sophisticated palates, our recipes will rekindle memories of celebrations past and awaken taste buds to new and entertaining times to come. We have included some practical and truly southern ways of entertaining—some tips passed down for generations and others new and unconventional for this generation. And when combined with our *Great Thyming Ideas* and *Party Planning Thymeline,* this cookbook will become part of your everyday entertaining as well as a reference for special occasions.

The members and associates of the Charity League of Paducah, Kentucky have carefully selected a wide variety of recipes and then double tested each one to ensure the highest quality, most precise accuracy, as well as appropriate presentation. Proceeds from the sale of this cookbook will benefit the children of Easter Seals West Kentucky along with the children and families of other support organizations in this community and region. Our most recent cookbook, *Seasons of Thyme,* has not only provided extensive financial assistance for these organizations for more than 22 years, but its success has also been the inspiration for *Thyme to Entertain*. Our theme of thyme carried throughout is meaningful as it is a reminder of the countless hours we have invested as volunteers on this project. We hope that it will be "thyme" well spent and will allow us to continue a long tradition of giving and support for those in need.

We want to thank you for purchasing *Thyme to Entertain* and for supporting the Charity League of Paducah, Kentucky. We hope this cookbook will become a part of your own mealtime memories and homespun hospitality.

So, take your thyme, savor, and enjoy!

The Charity League of Paducah, Kentucky

The **Charity League of Paducah, Kentucky** would like to thank our provisional, active, and associate members as well as their families and friends for their recipes, assistance in testing, editing, and prepublication work. We regret that we were unable to include all of the recipes submitted due to duplication, space constraints, and need for variety.

Our special thanks goes to **Jane Bright** for providing all of the artwork, **Pat Brockenborough** for historical research and editorial support, **Jane Gamble, Claire Key, and Ann Wurth** for proofreading, and local designer, **Laura Kauffman,** for her party planning expertise. We deeply appreciate the help of these people. Without their time, support, and efforts, *Thyme to Entertain* would not have been possible.

1999–2000 CHARITY LEAGUE MEMBERS

Carolyn Allen

Holli Brockenborough, *Public Relations*

Mary Buchanan, *Section Editor*

Laurie Carner

Kimberly Carr

Shelbye Coleman

Janet Colgan

Tonya Danesh

Heather Denton

Kim Eickholz

Julie Farmer, *Proofreading*

Patti Fletcher

Carol Gault

Susan Golightly

Sid Hancock, *Section Editor*

Claudia Hawkins

Amy Holland

Kelly Housman

Mary Katz, *Coordinating Chair and Editor*

Gena Karnes

Ellen Loughlin

Kelly McNulty, *Editorial Editor*

Laurie Miller

Deanna Minton

Kelly Morgan, *Marketing Chair*

Nancye Mullaney, *Section Editor*

Penny Orth, *Section Editor*

Connie Overstreet

Shannon Overstreet

Victoria Parrish

Karen Petter, *Food Chair*

Tammy Potter

Debbie Reynolds

Kim Rust

Kristi Schaaf

Ashley Shadoan, *Recipe Selection*

Angie Shannon, *Design*

Darla Sims, *Storyline Editor*

Kris Straub

Stacey Swift

Mary Lynn Thompson, *Testing Chair and Treasurer*

Jennifer Thompson

Lisa Wilkins

Maria Wilke

Kelly Workman

Thanks also to the many wonderful husbands who served as taste testers as well as babysitters during the long hours and late nights of production of this cookbook.

CONTRIBUTING ASSOCIATES

Kitty Anderson
Marian Bates
Charlene Beasley
Nancy W. Black
Ann Boyd
Beverly Bradley
Carol Bright
Jane Bright
Paula Bright
Pat Brockenborough
Brenda Brown
Denise Brown
Connie Byrd
Velma Carlton
Libby Cary
Olivia Cave
Phyllis Clymer
Robbin Cox
Lisa Craft
Jan Crawford
Sheila Cruse
Kerry Dallam
Ann Denton
Betty Edwards
Elizabeth Edwards
Karen Edwards
Rose Ann Fiorita
Kim Ford
Jeane Framptom
Carol Franks

Jane Gamble
Beth Garey
Judy Green
Paula Grubbs
Juliette Grumley
Laura Haas
Susan Hancock
Carol Hank
Jo Ann Hank
Julia Harper
Sueann Hely
Patricia Hines
Imogene Igert
Dorene Ivy
Roxie Jarvis
Cindy Jones
Margaret Kaltenbach
Mary Louise Katterjohn
Claire Key
Brenda Kunsman
Amy Lane
Renee Martin
Ruth McDowell
Mary McKewon
Lupe McMillan
Christy Meisenheimer
Sally Michelson
Glenda Miller
Robin Mills
Bonnie Moss
Carol Myre

Theresa Owens
Kayla Page
Caroline Parrish
Peggy Paxton
Beatrix Petter
Betty Polashock
Debbie Powell
Lucinda Ragland
Lana Rasche
Julie Rieke
Mary D. Rieke
Lucia Robertson
Kathy Schell
Meme Simmons
Connie Smith
Jane Smith
Sarah S. Stransky
Debe Sullivan
Sandy Swann
Debbie Taylor
Sara Tick
Joyce Titsworth
Judy Warmath
Lucy Weil
Mary Sue Whithrow
Roseann Whiting
Bette Whitlow
MeMe Wiley
Ann Wurth
Ginny Young
Katy Zaninovich

Table of Contents

Thyme to Entertain

GOOD FOOD AND
SOUTHERN HOSPITALITY

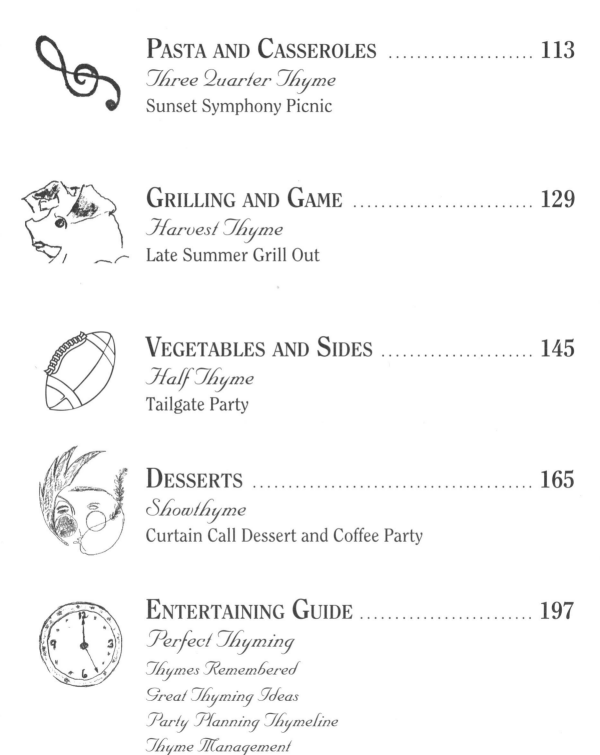

APPETIZERS AND BEVERAGES

Post Thyme

Post Thyme

Take from the cold spring, some water, pure as the angels are; mix it with sugar till it seems like oil. Then take a glass and crush your mint in it with a spoon. Crush it around the border of the glass and leave no place untouched. Then throw the mint away; it is a sacrifice. Fill the glass with cracked ice; pour in the quantity of bourbon which you want. It trickles slowly through the ice. Let it have time to cool, then pour your sugared water over it. No spoon is needed; no stirring allowed. Just let it stand a moment, so that the one who drinks may find taste and odor at one draught.

And that, my friend, is one heck of a fine mint julep.

Irvin S. Cobb

The Kentucky Derby is arguably the most exciting and popular thorough-bred horse race in the country. In Kentucky, the race, held on the first Saturday in May, takes precedence over all other sporting events. It is a celebration not just because it is the first of the prestigious Triple Crown thoroughbred races, but also because it is party *thyme* in the Bluegrass. Commemorating this century old tradition, equestrian lovers enjoy festivals, balls, parades, dinners, luncheons, and brunches.

Paducah is 225 miles from Churchill Downs, where the Derby is run, but certainly close enough to take part in the excitement. The race is viewed on television by Derby lovers ranging from small groups of friends to large gatherings. As guests arrive early in the afternoon to study racing forms and place their wagers in betting pools, the host passes hors d'oeuvres and beverages.

Mint juleps are the traditional Derby drink. It is strong and cloyingly sweet, but most revelers agree that at least one should be consumed on this occasion.

After the race, supper is served. The meal is usually potluck, with guests bringing their very best versions of salads, casseroles, and desserts. No ordinary covered-dish meal is this; the food is always elegant and special.

Derby Day is an exciting time in Kentucky. In Paducah, it's *Thyme to Entertain*.

Derby Day Celebration

The Perfect Mint Julep

Mushroom Puffs

Party Cheese Straws

Raspberry Honey Mustard Pork Tenderloin
on Savory Yeast Rolls

Roasted Rosemary New Potatoes

Green Bean Bundles

"Run for the Roses" Derby Pie

Almond Crunch Cookies

Post Thyme Party Tips

A Sure Bet—

WIN–over guests with unique and handmade invitations in the shape of horseshoes.
PLACE–settings can be trimmed with jersey silks or racing forms.
SHOW–creativeness with flowers in riding boots.

Madeira Mushrooms

Madeira wine, traditionally a dessert wine, adds just the right touch of sweetness to this outstanding appetizer.

18 large mushrooms (stems
    removed and reserved)

8 tablespoons butter, divided

9 tablespoons minced green
    onion (tops included)

1½ tablespoons vegetable oil

½ cup Madeira wine

4-5 tablespoons heavy cream

4½ tablespoons dry bread
    crumbs

½ cup grated Swiss cheese

¾ teaspoon tarragon

Salt and pepper to taste

- Preheat oven to 375°.
- Place mushroom caps in a buttered 9 x 13-inch pan. Melt 5 tablespoons butter; brush over mushrooms.
- Chop mushroom stems and sauté with onions in remaining butter and oil.
- Add Madeira wine and boil rapidly until slightly reduced.
- Remove from heat and stir in remaining ingredients.
- Spoon into mushroom caps.
- Bake for 15 to 20 minutes.

Yields 18 mushrooms

Hot Bacon Melba Rounds

Easy and delicious!

½ pound bacon, cooked and
    crumbled

1 cup shredded processed cheese
    loaf

¼ cup margarine, softened

2 teaspoons caraway seeds

1 box plain Melba toast rounds

- Mix crumbled bacon with cheese, margarine and caraway seeds.
- Spread on Melba rounds and broil for 4 minutes or until cheese is hot and bubbling (watch so it does not burn).
- Serve hot.
- Note: Mixture can be prepared ahead and put on Melba rounds until ready to broil.

Yields 50 appetizers

Prosciutto-Wrapped Asparagus

12 thin slices prosciutto, cut into halves

24 asparagus spears, cut to 4 inches and lightly steamed

½ teaspoon salt

½ teaspoon fresh cracked black pepper

- Preheat oven to 325°.
- Wrap each asparagus spear with a slice of prosciutto, starting at the tip and ending at the end of the spear.
- Arrange spears on a baking sheet.
- Sprinkle with salt and pepper.
- Heat for 4 to 5 minutes or until hot.
- Serve immediately.

Yields 8 to 10

Crispy Pesto Shrimp

12 jumbo shrimp, cooked and peeled

6 slices white bread

¼ cup butter, softened

1 clove garlic

1 tablespoon plus 1 teaspoon prepared pesto sauce

1 teaspoon finely grated lemon rind

¼ teaspoon salt

¼ teaspoon ground black pepper

- Cut each shrimp in half. Cut crusts off bread. Using a rolling pin, roll each piece of bread flat.
- In a small bowl, beat butter until smooth. Stir in garlic, pesto sauce, lemon rind, salt and pepper. Beat until smooth and well blended.
- Spread both sides of bread slices with butter mixture; cut each slice into four triangles. Fold two points over shrimp half and secure with wooden toothpick.
- Arrange on a grill pan and broil until bread is lightly browned. Watch carefully.

Yields 24 appetizers

"The company makes the feast."

— a French proverb

Green Chile Pie

A great appetizer that can be prepared on the spur of the moment! Men love this one!

3 (4 ounce) cans chopped green
    chiles, drained

2 cups grated sharp cheddar
    cheese

2 eggs, beaten

2 tablespoons water

- Preheat oven to 350°.
- Butter a 9-inch glass pie plate or a 9-inch quiche dish.
- Cover bottom with chiles then layer with cheese.
- Beat eggs with water. Pour over cheese and chiles.
- Bake for 35 to 40 minutes or until lightly browned.
- Serve with shredded wheat crackers.

Serves 6

Mushroom Puffs

2 (8 ounce) cans refrigerated
    crescent dinner rolls

1 (8 ounce) package cream
    cheese, softened

1 (4 ounce) can mushrooms
    (stems and pieces included),
    drained

2 green onions, chopped

1 teaspoon seasoned salt

1 large egg, beaten

2 tablespoons poppy seeds

- Preheat oven to 375°.
- Lay out crescent roll dough and press perforations to seal.
- Mix cream cheese, mushrooms, onions and salt; spread over dough.
- Roll up jelly roll fashion and slice into 1-inch pieces.
- Brush with egg; sprinkle with poppy seeds and bake for 10 minutes.
- Serve hot.
- Note: It is easier to slice roll if you put it in the freezer for 15 minutes before slicing.

Yields 32 puffs

Almond Pinecones

1¼ cups whole almonds

1 (8 ounce) package cream
  cheese

½ cup mayonnaise

5 bacon slices, cooked crisp and
  crumbled

1 tablespoon chopped green
  onion

½ teaspoon dill weed

⅛ teaspoon pepper

Pine sprigs for garnish

- Toast almonds.
- Combine cream cheese and mayonnaise. Mix well.
- Add bacon, onions, dill weed and pepper. Mix together and cover. Chill overnight.
- Form into two pinecone shapes joined at the top. Place almonds on outside to resemble pinecones.
- Garnish the top of each pinecone with a sprig of pine.

Serves 10 to 12

Extraordinary Crab Dip

Excellent for holiday cocktail parties!

½ cup butter

1 large yellow onion, finely chopped

1 bunch green onions, chopped
  (reserve some for garnish)

1 (8 ounce) package cream
  cheese (do not use low-fat)

1 (10.5 ounce) can cream of
  celery soup

1 pound fresh or canned crabmeat

¼ cup half-and-half

1 clove fresh garlic, minced

1 tablespoon fresh lemon juice

2 tablespoons Worcestershire
  sauce

1 tablespoon hot sauce

¼ teaspoon cayenne pepper

¼ teaspoon crab boil

Salt and pepper to taste

- In a large skillet, melt butter. Add yellow and green onions; sauté on low heat.
- Blend together cream cheese and celery soup; add to onions.
- Add crabmeat and slowly pour in half-and-half.
- Add remaining ingredients and continue to heat on low until heated throughout, stirring frequently.
- Pour into chafing dish, garnish with chopped green onions. Serve with fresh, sliced baguette or crackers.

Serves 20

15

Feta Triangles

3 large eggs

1 (3 ounce) package cream cheese, softened

8 ounces ricotta cheese

8 ounces feta cheese

1 (16 ounce) package frozen phyllo pastry, thawed

1 cup unsalted butter, melted

- Preheat oven to 375°.
- Beat eggs at medium speed for 1 minute; beat in cheeses.
- Unfold phyllo and cover with a slightly damp towel to prevent pastry from drying out.
- Place 1 phyllo sheet on a flat surface covered with wax paper. Cut lengthwise into four strips. Brush top of each strip with melted butter. Fold strips in half lengthwise and brush with butter.
- Place 1 teaspoon cheese mixture at base of each strip; fold right bottom corner over to form a triangle. Continue folding back and forth into a triangle, gently pressing corners together. Repeat folding for remaining three strips.
- Place triangles, seam side down on ungreased baking sheets and brush with butter. Repeat procedure with remaining phyllo sheets.
- Bake for 15 minutes or until golden brown.
- Note: Triangles may be prepared ahead and frozen for up to two weeks. Bake as directed without thawing.

Yields 80 triangles

"Plan, plan, plan…so that you are not in the kitchen the whole time after your guests arrive. Do as much as possible ahead, leaving nothing to chance. Make a checklist and check it off as you do it."

Tantalizing Baguettes

Great little edibles!

1 large baguette, sliced
6 tablespoons butter, softened
¼ cup olive oil
24 cherry tomatoes, sliced
1 (8 ounce) block fresh
    mozzarella, cut into 24 slices
Salt and pepper to taste
24 fresh basil leaves

- Cut baguette diagonally into 24 slices.
- Spread both sides of baguette slices with butter and a brush of olive oil.
- Arrange slices on baking sheets and broil for 1 to 2 minutes. Turn slices over and repeat. Cool.
- Thinly slice cherry tomatoes.
- Slice mozzarella in ¼-inch slices.
- Toss tomatoes, mozzarella, salt, pepper and 1 teaspoon olive oil together. Let stand 10 minutes.
- Place mozzarella slices and tomatoes on baguette slices. Top with a sprig of fresh basil.
- Salt and pepper to taste.

Yields 24 appetizers

Sausage Stuffed Mushrooms

Quick and easy!

24 large fresh mushrooms
1 pound pork sausage, cooked
4 tablespoons finely chopped
    fresh parsley
1 clove garlic, minced
1 cup freshly grated Parmesan
    cheese, divided

- Preheat oven to 350°.
- Clean mushrooms and remove stems.
- Cook sausage according to package directions.
- Finely chop mushroom stems and place in large mixing bowl. Add parsley, garlic, ¼ cup Parmesan cheese and sausage. Mix well.
- Stuff mushroom caps and place on a cookie sheet.
- Bake for 15 to 20 minutes. Do not overcook since sausage is already cooked.
- Remove and place on a serving dish; sprinkle with remaining Parmesan cheese.

Yields 24 mushrooms

Bacon-Wrapped Waterchestnuts

Easy and tasty!

½ cup soy sauce
2 cups sugar, divided
4 (8 ounce) cans whole water
    chestnuts, drained
2 pounds bacon

- Combine soy sauce and ½ cup sugar, mixing well.
- Soak water chestnuts in mixture for 30 minutes; drain.
- Preheat oven to 400°.
- Roll water chestnuts in remaining sugar.
- Cut each bacon strip in half.
- Wrap a bacon strip around each water chestnut; secure with a toothpick.
- Bake for 15 to 20 minutes.
- Cover with foil and refrigerate until serving time.
- Broil 5 minutes; drain on paper towels before serving.

Yields 60 appetizers

Bacon-Wrapped Shrimp

Quick and easy!

12 large shrimp, peeled (leave
    tail shells) and deveined
1 garlic clove, minced
¼ cup lemon juice
1 tablespoon lime juice
2 tablespoons soy sauce
Cracked black pepper to taste
6 bacon slices, halved
12 small wooden skewers

- Wash and prepare shrimp.
- Mix garlic, lemon juice, lime juice and soy sauce in a large bowl.
- Pat shrimp dry and add to bowl.
- Let shrimp marinate for 30 minutes.
- Soak skewers in water for 30 minutes.
- Remove shrimp and wrap bacon slice around the center of each shrimp.
- Thread each shrimp onto a skewer through the tail. Sprinkle with black pepper.
- Grill on medium-high heat for 4 to 5 minutes or until
- Serve warm.

Variation: Can place two shrimps on a skewer for a heavier appetizer.

Yields 12 appetizers

Miniature Sausage Quiches

Great for a luncheon or bridal shower!

1 pound sausage
½ cup chopped green onion
⅓ cup chopped green pepper
1½ cups grated cheddar cheese
1 tablespoon flour
1 cup evaporated milk
1 tablespoon parsley
¾ teaspoon seasoned salt
½ teaspoon garlic salt
2 eggs, beaten
1 unbaked pie crust

- Preheat oven to 350°.
- Brown sausage, green onions and green peppers in a skillet. Drain and set aside.
- In a small bowl, combine cheese and flour. Set aside.
- Mix milk, parsley, salts and beaten eggs together. Set aside.
- Grease and flour a mini-muffin pan.
- Remove unbaked pie crust from package. Lay on a lightly floured surface and roll out slightly. Using a 2-inch round cookie cutter or drinking glass, cut out circles of dough and press them into the mini-muffin pan. Place a spoonful of sausage mixture in each cup followed by a generous pinch of cheese mixture. When complete, pour milk mixture into cup holes to fill. Bake for 15 minutes or until firm.
- Note: This dish can be prepared ahead and frozen. Reheat to serve.

Variation: Can also be prepared as one dish. Pour mixture into an unbaked pie crust. Bake at 350° for 25 to 30 minutes or until crust is brown. Serves 6.

Yields 2 dozen

"One of the cutest ideas I've seen for casual dinner parties uses a Polaroid camera. As guests arrive, their pictures are taken and then later used as place cards. It's fun to see people looking for their places."

Avocado Salmon Rolls

A sophisticated yet simple hors d'oeuvre to serve at your next cocktail party!

Filling:
4 ounces cream cheese, softened
1 avocado, peeled and mashed
2 tablespoons chopped fresh dill
2 small tomatoes, peeled, seeded
   and chopped
½ teaspoon ground black pepper

Salmon:
6 ounces smoked salmon slices
6 slices rye bread
2 tablespoons butter
Lemon twists for garnish
Dill sprigs for garnish

- To prepare filling, beat cream cheese in a bowl until smooth. Stir in mashed avocado until blended. Add dill, tomatoes and pepper; stir gently.
- Place mixture in a pastry bag fitted with a ½-inch nozzle.
- Cut smoked salmon in 40 (1½ x 1-inch) rectangles.
- Pipe a length of cheese mixture across the top of the short edge of each salmon rectangle and roll up.
- Spread rye bread with butter. Cut into 40 rectangles to fit salmon rolls. Place salmon on each piece of bread.
- Garnish with lemon twists and dill sprigs.

Yields 40 rolls

Caramel Brie Cheese

Great for small gatherings!

2 tablespoons butter, melted
¾ cup brown sugar
¼ cup light corn syrup
1 tablespoon flour
¼ cup milk
1 (15 ounce) package Brie cheese
½ cup coarsely chopped pecans,
   for garnish

- Melt butter; add brown sugar and corn syrup. Mix well.
- Stir in flour and milk. Bring to a boil then reduce heat and simmer for 5 minutes, stirring constantly. Remove from heat.
- Remove rind from top of Brie cheese. Microwave Brie for 45 seconds to soften cheese in the middle.
- Pour caramel mixture over Brie cheese and top with pecans.
- Serve with crackers.
- Note: Caramel mixture may be made ahead and microwave just before serving.

Serves 6 to 8

Sun-Dried Tomato and Pesto Terrine

First layer:

1½ pounds cream cheese,
   softened

2 cups butter, softened

2 teaspoons black pepper

½ teaspoon salt

Second layer:

2 cups tightly packed fresh basil

½ cup pine nuts, toasted

½ cup grated Parmesan cheese

¼ cup minced garlic

½ cup olive oil

1 teaspoon salt

2 teaspoons black pepper

Third layer:

2 cups sun-dried tomatoes,
   drained

1 tablespoon chopped marjoram

2 teaspoons minced garlic

1 teaspoon black pepper

- Purée the ingredients for the first layer in a food processor until smooth. Reserve at room temperature.
- Purée the ingredients for the second layer in a food processor until almost smooth. Reserve at room temperature.
- Blend the ingredients for the third layer in a food processor until smooth. Reserve at room temperature.
- Line a 4 to 6 cup serving bowl with plastic wrap (allow a 2-inch overhang). Make the wrap as wrinkle free as possible.
- Begin filling the bowl with alternating layers of ingredients as follows:
  ½ inch: layer one
  ¼ inch: layer two
  ½ inch: layer one
  ¼ inch: layer three; repeat.
- To eliminate air pockets, tap base of bowl on a table after each layer.
- After adding the last layer, which should be the first layer, cover with plastic wrap and refrigerate at least 4 hours.
- To serve, invert onto serving plastic and then onto a serving platter.
- Once unmolded, remove plastic wrap. Arrange your favorite crackers, toasts or breads around terrine.
- Note: Arrange fresh basil leaves on top of terrine and serve with garlic toasted Melba rounds.

Serves 15 to 20

"If you do not have a warming tray…get one!
Particularly if you have only one oven!"

Chutney Cheese Spread

Great for autumn parties! Serve in a hollowed pumpkin.

4 cups finely grated cheddar
  cheese
4 cloves garlic, minced
2 (3 ounce) packages cream
  cheese, softened
1 tablespoon curry powder
¾ cup chopped scallions (reserve
  some for garnish)
4 tablespoons mayonnaise
1 (9 ounce) jar mango chutney

- Combine all ingredients in a large bowl; mix well.
- Serve in a hollowed pumpkin.
- Garnish with a few chopped scallions.

Serves 20

Crab and Cheese Piroque

1 loaf French bread
1 cup mayonnaise
1 bunch green onions, chopped
2 (6 ounce) cans crabmeat,
  (drain only one can)
2 cups grated cheddar cheese
1 teaspoon garlic powder
2 teaspoons red pepper
Paprika for garnish

- Preheat oven to 350°.
- Hollow out French bread loaf.
- Combine mayonnaise, onions, crabmeat, cheese, garlic powder, and red pepper in mixing bowl.
- Scoop cheese mixture into hollowed bread loaf. Sprinkle with paprika if desired.
- Bake on a cookie sheet for 30 minutes or until cheese becomes slightly browned and bubbly.
- Serve with crackers.

Serves 15 to 20

Artichoke Seafood Bake

2 (14 ounce) cans artichoke
  hearts
1 pound fresh crabmeat
12 tablespoons butter, divided
½ pound fresh mushrooms
Salt and pepper to taste
2 pounds shrimp
8 tablespoons flour
3 cups half-and-half
2 tablespoons Worcestershire
  sauce
½ cup dry sherry
¾ cup grated Parmesan cheese
Lemon
Paprika

- Preheat oven to 350°.
- Drain and quarter artichokes; place in a buttered 9 x 13-inch casserole dish.
- Spread crabmeat over artichokes.
- Sauté mushrooms in 4 tablespoons butter. Salt and pepper mushrooms to taste.
- Spread mushrooms in casserole dish over crabmeat. Layer shrimp on top of mushrooms.
- Melt 8 tablespoons butter. Slowly stir in flour. Cook over low heat for 3 to 5 minutes.
- Whisk in half-and-half; cook until thick. Add Worcestershire sauce and sherry. Pour sauce over casserole.
- Sprinkle with Parmesan, paprika and lemon.
- Bake for 25 to 30 minutes.

Serves 8

Glazed Raspberry Cheese Ball

2 cups shredded cheddar cheese
2 cups shredded American brick
  cheese
8 green onions, chopped
1 cup chopped pecans
4 tablespoons mayonnaise
1½ cups raspberry preserves

- Mix cheeses, onions, pecans and mayonnaise.
- Turn onto wax paper and form into a ball. Cover and refrigerate, chilling well.
- When ready to serve, invert onto a serving plate.
- Frost top and sides with raspberry preserves.
- Serve with crackers.
- Note: Cheese ball can be made several days in advance and frosted with preserves just before serving.

Serves 10 to 12

Layered Cheese Torte

Interesting and different. Great for cheese lovers!

First layer:

1 (10 ounce) package shredded
    sharp cheddar cheese

1 cup chopped pecans

1 medium sweet onion, chopped

Second layer:

1 (8 ounce) cream cheese, softened

⅓ cup chutney

Third layer:

1 (10 ounce) package frozen
    chopped spinach, cooked and
    well drained

1 (8 ounce) package cream
    cheese, softened

¼ teaspoon garlic powder

⅛ teaspoon oregano

⅛ teaspoon basil

Pepper to taste

Celery seed to taste

Nutmeg to taste

- Spray bottom of soufflé dish or an 8 ounce plastic whipped topping container generously with nonstick cooking spray.
- Combine first layer ingredients. Divide this mixture in half. Pat first half into dish.
- Combine second layer ingredients. Spread this over the first layer.
- Combine third layer ingredients. Spread on top of second layer.
- Using the other half of the first layer, spread on top of the third layer and pat.
- Chill before serving. Can be made one or two days ahead.
- When ready to serve, turn dish over onto plate. Serve with crackers.

Serves 12 to 15

Holiday Pumpkin Dip

This is a good holiday treat!

1 (8 ounce) package cream
    cheese, softened

½ cup light brown sugar

½ cup canned pumpkin

2 teaspoons maple syrup

½ teaspoon cinnamon

- Combine cream cheese, brown sugar, pumpkin, maple syrup and cinnamon in a mixing bowl. Mix until smooth.
- Serving idea: Hollow out a small pumpkin or gourd. Line inside with plastic wrap and fill with dip. Sprinkle top with a dash of nutmeg and serve with apple slices or ginger snaps.

Serves 8 to 10

The Best Apple Dip

This recipe is great to bring to a casual gathering. Enjoyed by adults and kids alike.

1 (8 ounce) package cream
 cheese, softened
⅓ cup brown sugar
¼ cup sugar
1 teaspoon vanilla
1 (7.5 ounce) package almond
 brickle chips
4 red apples
4 yellow apples
¼ cup lemon juice

- Combine cream cheese, and brown sugar; let stand 10 minutes.
- Stir in sugar, vanilla and almond brickle chips.
- Core and slice apples. Dip slices in lemon juice to prevent browning.
- Arrange apple slices and dip on a serving platter.
- Note: This can be prepared ahead and refrigerated in airtight containers.

Serves 10 to 12

Antipasto Appetizer

1 (8 ounce) block sharp cheddar
 cheese, cut into bite-size
 cubes
1 (8 ounce) block Swiss cheese,
 cut into bite-size cubes
1 (8 ounce) block pepper jack
 cheese, cut into bite-size
 cubes
2 (6 ounce) cans large pitted
 whole black olives, drained
2 (14 ounce) cans quartered
 artichoke hearts, drained
1 (16 ounce) package polska
 kielbasa or smoked sausage,
 sliced into ½-inch thick coins
1 (8 ounce) bottle of zesty Italian
 dressing

- Combine first six ingredients.
- Pour dressing over mixture, tossing well.
- Refrigerate a minimum of 3 hours.
- Serve in a pretty serving bowl. Use toothpicks for easier pickup.

Variation: Prepare as directed. Grease a 9 x 13-inch pan. Layer bottom of pan with cooked rotini noodles. Pour antipasto over noodles and bake at 350° for 20 minutes or until cheeses are melted. Top with grated Parmesan cheese.

Serves 10 to 12

Spicy Taco Dip

A must for tailgate parties or backyard get-togethers!

2 (8 ounce) packages cream
   cheese, softened

1 (8 ounce) container sour
   cream

1 package dry taco seasoning mix

2 ripe avocados

1 package guacamole seasoning
   mix*

1 (15 ounce) can refried beans

1 (8 ounce) jar hot salsa, drained
   of excess juice

1 cup shredded cheddar cheese

1 (4.5 ounce) can chopped green
   chiles, drained

2 medium tomatoes, diced

1 (4.5 ounce) can sliced black
   olives, drained

- Mix together cream cheese, sour cream and taco seasoning.
- Peel avocados and prepare as directed on package of guacamole seasoning mix.
- Spread refried beans onto an 11-inch round x 1½-inch deep serving platter.
- Layer with remaining ingredients: cream cheese mixture, guacamole, salsa, cheese, chopped chiles, diced tomatoes and black olives.
- Refrigerate until served. Serve with tortilla chips.

*Available in produce section of most grocery stores.

Serves 15 to 20

South of the Border Salsa

12 Roma tomatoes, finely chopped

3 green onions, finely chopped

½ small purple onion, finely
   chopped

½ bunch cilantro, finely chopped

1 jalapeño pepper, finely chopped

2 lemons, juiced

1 lime, juiced

1 teaspoon garlic, crushed

Salt to taste

- Mix all ingredients together in a large mixing bowl.
- Refrigerate for 1 hour.

Serves 8

New Orleans Finger Sandwiches

Great little pick up for a luncheon!

1 cup mayonnaise

1 dash Tabasco sauce

¼ teaspoon dry mustard

½ teaspoon lemon juice

1 dash Worcestershire sauce

White pepper to taste

1 cup fresh spinach, washed and drained

8 slices bacon, cooked crisp and crumbled

1 loaf wheat or white sandwich bread, quartered with crusts removed

- Combine mayonnaise, Tabasco sauce, dry mustard, lemon juice, Worcestershire sauce and white pepper.
- Cut spinach into small pieces; add to mayonnaise mixture along with bacon crumbs. Mix well.
- Spread on bread quarters to make sandwiches or serve as a dip with crackers.
- Note: For a special touch, use homemade mayonnaise.

Serves 6 to 10

Teatime Sandwiches

1 (8 ounce) package cream cheese, softened

2 tablespoons mayonnaise

½ tablespoon finely chopped green onion

Dash of red pepper

Dash of hot sauce

½ cup peeled, seeded and grated cucumber

24 slices thin, white sandwich bread

Garnishes:

Fresh cucumber wedges

Fresh dill

Cherry tomato halves

- Combine cream cheese, mayonnaise, green onion, red pepper and hot sauce in a large bowl. Beat at medium speed until smooth. Set aside.
- Drain grated cucumber on paper towels, carefully patting out excess moisture. Fold into cream cheese mixture and set aside.
- Using 2- or 3-inch cookie cutter shapes, cut bread into desired shapes. Spread bread top with filling. Garnish with cucumber, dill and cherry tomato halves.
- Note: This recipe may be doubled and filling may be prepared an hour ahead. Do not freeze.

Yields 2 dozen

Marinated Shrimp

Excellent served on slices of buttered French bread!

5 pounds shrimp, cooked, peeled
    and deveined
1 purple onion, sliced into rings
1 (3 ounce) jar capers, drained
3 garlic cloves, minced
1 bunch fresh cilantro, chopped
4 green jalapeños, seeded and
    chopped
1 (4.5 ounce) jar marinated
    mushrooms, drained and
    sliced
2 (6.5 ounce) jars marinated
    artichoke hearts, drained and
    chopped
1 lemon, thinly sliced (seeds
    removed)

Marinade:
¾ cup fresh lemon juice
¾ cup white vinegar
1½ cups oil
Salt and pepper to taste
1 teaspoon dry mustard
¼ cup sugar

- Combine first nine ingredients in a large bowl.
- Combine all marinade ingredients in a separate bowl.
- Pour over shrimp and marinate for 1 to 2 hours in the refrigerator.
- Note: Serve on leaf lettuce as a side dish or in a serving bowl for an appetizer.

Serves 20 as an appetizer

> "When I am in a rush and have to use prepared party platters, I make sure that I buy assorted garnishes such as parsley, lettuce, lemon, or herbs and transfer the food to my own glass or silver platters. I think my guests appreciate my efforts to have a pretty table."

Party Cheese Straws

8 ounces extra-sharp cheddar
  cheese, softened
½ cup butter, softened
½ teaspoon salt
¾ teaspoon red pepper
1½ cups flour

- Preheat oven to 325°.
- Blend softened cheese and butter in food processor until smooth.
- Add seasonings and flour.
- Mix until dough is pliable.
- Press through cookie press onto ungreased cookie sheet.
- Bake for 20 to 25 minutes. Watch carefully while baking!
- Let cool on pan.
- Break into desired sized pieces.
- Note: If cookie press is not available, roll into small balls and press with a fork.

Serves 20 to 30

Spicy Pecans

2 cups water
2 cups plus 1 teaspoon sugar,
  divided
¼ teaspoon plus ⅛ teaspoon
  cayenne pepper, divided
2 cups pecan halves
2 tablespoons butter
½ teaspoon salt
¼ teaspoon cinnamon

- Combine water, 2 cups sugar and ¼ teaspoon cayenne pepper in a medium saucepan.
- Cook over medium heat, stirring occasionally, for five minutes and when mixture comes to a boil and thickens.
- Add pecan halves and cook for an additional 5 minutes, stirring often.
- Drain pecans in a colander.
- Preheat oven to 350°.
- Melt butter on a large cookie sheet. Spread coated pecan halves onto cookie sheet and bake 12 to 15 minutes until pecans turn dark in color.
- Combine remaining sugar and cayenne pepper, salt and cinnamon. Toss pecans with mixture. Cool.

Yields 2 cups

Cherry Tomatoes with Blue Cheese

24 medium cherry tomatoes,
   washed and dried
4 ounces blue cheese
1 tablespoon red wine vinegar
1 tablespoon olive oil
¼ teaspoon dried basil
Salt and pepper

- Cut tops of tomatoes with a serrated knife.
- Scoop out pulp with a serrated spoon or a melon scoop.
- Blend blue cheese, vinegar, olive oil and basil in a bowl.
- Sprinkle inside of tomatoes with salt and pepper.
- Using the small side of a melon scoop, stuff each tomato with blue cheese mixture, being careful not to tear tomato.
- Sprinkle tops with salt and pepper.

Yields 24 tomatoes

Mini New Potatoes Stuffed with Dill

18 bite-size new potatoes
4 bacon slices
¼ cup sour cream
2 tablespoons cream cheese
½ teaspoon dill weed
¼ teaspoon garlic powder
¼ teaspoon salt
¼ teaspoon pepper

- Cook potatoes in boiling water for 20 minutes or until tender. Rinse and cool potatoes.
- Cook bacon until crisp. Crumble into small pieces.
- Cut the tops off the potatoes and scoop out the middle of potatoes; place pulp in a small bowl. Stir in bacon, sour cream, cream cheese, dill weed and remaining spices.
- Carefully stuff each potato.
- Serve hot or cold.
- Note: For best results, select potatoes the approximate size of cherry tomatoes.

Yields 18 potatoes

Hot Bacon Cheese Bites

½ cup grated sharp cheddar

6 slices bacon, cooked and crumbled

1 small onion, chopped

¼ cup slivered almonds

1 cup mayonnaise

2 teaspoons Worcestershire sauce

Salt and pepper to taste

10 slices white sandwich bread

- Preheat oven to 400°.
- Mix all ingredients except bread.
- Remove crusts from bread and quarter slices.
- Spread mixture on bread quarters.
- Arrange on two cookie sheets.
- Cook for 10 minutes at 400°.
- Serve immediately.

Yields 40 triangles

"Packing two coolers is a necessity when entertaining on the go. Use one cooler that will be opened frequently and pack the other with perishables that will be used later."

Tiny Blossoms

Great for bridal and baby showers! Elegant and easy!

20 large fresh strawberries,
  washed

1 (3 ounce) package cream
  cheese, softened

2 tablespoons finely chopped
  walnuts

2 tablespoons confectioners'
  sugar

1 teaspoon mandarin liqueur

- Chop two strawberries. Set aside.
- Cut the stem end of each strawberry (so it can stand easily).
- Cut each strawberry into four wedges starting from the tips but not cutting all the way through.
- Beat cream cheese until soft. Mix in diced strawberries, walnuts, confectioners' sugar and liqueur. Gently spoon or pipe mixture into strawberry tips. Be careful not to tear berries!
- Note: Have extra strawberries on hand because some strawberries may tear. This recipe can be doubled.

Yields 18 blossoms

Bold and Spicy Bloody Marys

1 (1 liter) bottle hot and spicy
   Bloody Mary mix
2 tablespoons Tabasco sauce
2 tablespoons Rendezvous®
   Famous Seasoning*
2 limes, juiced
6 tablespoons Worcestershire
   sauce
1 teaspoon celery salt
1½ cups vodka

Garnishes:
Celery stalks
Limes wedges
Rendezvous® Famous
   Seasoning*

- Combine all ingredients in pitcher.
- Mix well.
- Serve over ice in a pewter Jefferson cup or julep cup.
- Garnish with celery stalk, lime wedge and sprinkle of Rendezvous® Famous Seasoning.

Serves 6

*Available in the condiment section of most grocery stores.

Patio Peach Daiquiri

2 ounces premium brand lime
   juice*
4 ounces rum
3-4 tablespoons sugar
2 pitted fresh peaches, washed
   but not peeled
Ice

- Place lime juice, rum, sugar and peaches in a blender.
- Add ice until blender is filled.
- Blend until smooth. Serve in mint julep cups.

Strawberries may be substituted for peaches.

Serves 5 to 6

*Available in specialty stores.

Grand Mimosa

This is a great family tradition for Christmas brunch!

½ cup orange-flavored liqueur
¼ cup sugar
1 bottle champagne, chilled
2 cups freshly squeezed orange
   juice

- Pour liqueur into a small bowl or saucer.
- Put sugar on a saucer and dip the rim of the champagne glass into the liqueur, then in the sugar.
- Carefully fill each glass with ¾ champagne and ¼ orange juice.
- Add a dash of orange liqueur to each glass.

Serves 8

Party Margaritas

1 (6 ounce) can frozen
   lemonade
1 (6 ounce) can frozen limeade
1½ cups premium brand
   tequila, divided
⅔ cups orange-flavored liqueur
Ice
Lemons or limes for garnish

- Combine in blender: ½ can lemonade, ½ can limeade, ¾ cup tequila and ⅓ cup liqueur. Blend.
- Add enough ice to bring to 4 cup level. Process until smooth. Transfer blended mixture to container and repeat procedure with remaining ingredients.
- Garnish with lemons or limes.

Yields 2 quarts

Cranberry Slush

Great drink on the patio or for the Christmas holidays.

3 (12 ounce) cans frozen lemonade
   concentrate, thawed
36 ounces cranberry juice
3 cups rum
1 (1 liter) bottle lemon-lime soft
   drink

- Mix lemonade, cranberry juice and rum together, then freeze. Better if made at least 12 hours ahead.
- When frozen, spoon into glasses then add chilled lemon-lime soft drink. Best to use ⅔ cranberry mixture to ⅓ lemon-lime soft drink.
- Note: Can be prepared ahead.

Yields 12 to 15 drinks

Sweet Bourbon Slush

1 (12 ounce) can frozen
   lemonade
1 (6 ounce) can frozen orange
   juice
¾ cup sugar
2 cups bourbon
5 cups water
Mint leaves for garnish

- Thaw juices.
- Stir first five ingredients together and pour into a freezer container. Freeze overnight.
- Remove container from freezer 15 minutes before serving.
- Spoon into glasses and garnish with mint leaves.

Serves 6

Frosty Banana Punch

Kids and adults agree- this one is yummy!

6 bananas
1 (12 ounce) can frozen orange
   juice concentrate
1 (6 ounce) can frozen lemonade
1 quart pineapple juice
4½ cups water
2 cups sugar
1 (2 liter) lemon-lime soda or
   ginger ale

- In a blender, combine bananas, orange juice and lemonade. Blend.
- Add pineapple juice, water and sugar.
- Pour into a freezer container and freeze overnight.
- Remove container from freezer. Thaw 30 minutes or until slush-like.
- Add lemon-lime soda or ginger ale and stir.
- Serve in a punch bowl.

Serves 40

"When purchasing beverages, buy what you know to be good and always include non-alcoholic choices."

Wine Punch with Melon

1 cantaloupe
1 small watermelon
10 ounces dry white table wine
10 ounces sweet Riesling wine
16 ounces Asti wine
6 red grapes, sliced crosswise in
    half
6 green grapes, sliced crosswise
    in half

- Using a melon baller, scoop the cantaloupe and watermelon into balls. Place balls on a baking sheet. Make sure they do not touch one another. Freeze several hours or overnight.
- Mix wines in a large glass pitcher. Add grape slices and frozen cantaloupe and watermelon balls to pitcher and serve.

Serves 6

Festive Citrus Wassail

Wassail is Scandinavian for "may you be in good health" and is the perfect cup of cheer to share with friends when toasting the holidays.

1 (64 ounce) carton orange juice
1 (64 ounce) bottle apple juice
1 (32 ounce) bottle cranberry
    juice cocktail
1 (12 ounce) can frozen
    lemonade concentrate,
    thawed
3 (2 inch) sticks cinnamon
1 tablespoon whole cloves
2 oranges, sliced

- Combine juices, lemonade and cinnamon in a Dutch oven. Press cloves into orange slices and add to juice mixture.
- Simmer, uncovered, for 15 minutes or until heated thoroughly.
- Serve warm with a cinnamon stick or peppermint candy stick.
- Note: If desired, stir in 3 cups of bourbon with juices and cook as directed.

Yields 2 quarts

"My three rules for a perfect party…invite more people than you have room for, prepare more food than you think you need, and relax and enjoy your guests."

The Perfect Mint Julep

An essential for a derby party!

1 (1 liter) bottle Maker's Mark
  bourbon whiskey
1 bunch fresh mint
1 cup sugar
1 cup water
Crushed ice
Chilled silver tumblers, optional
Confectioners' sugar for garnish

- Wash and pat dry mint leaves.
- Place leaves in a bowl with just enough bourbon to cover leaves. Let soak for 15 minutes.
- Meanwhile, heat sugar and water in saucepan long enough to dissolve sugar. Be careful not to burn.
- Remove syrup from heat and cool.
- Remove leaves from bowl and place on clean cloth to drain.
- Fill each julep cup ½ full with crushed ice.
- Insert mint sprig and add more crushed ice.
- Add 1 to 2 tablespoons syrup to cup.
- Add 2½ ounces bourbon and jiggle with long-handled spoon. Do not stir!
- For garnish, sift a small amount of confectioners' sugar over top of drink and finish with a sprig of mint.
- Note: The syrup will keep indefinitely in the refrigerator. The 1 cup sugar and 1 cup water makes about 1 cup.

Yields 8 to 10 juleps

Red Sangria

2 bottles Chianti wine
6 lemons, (2) juiced and (4)
  thinly sliced
4 oranges, thinly sliced
6 peaches, peeled and cubed
½ cup brandy
8 tablespoons sugar
Club soda to taste (optional)
Fruit for garnish

- Mix all ingredients well; chill for several hours or overnight in a covered container.
- Pour into a glass pitcher or tall glasses with ice. Garnish with a piece of fruit.
- Note: Be sure to taste the fruit!

Serves 6

Iced Mint Tea

6 cups water
2 cups sugar
3 family-size tea bags
8-10 pieces of mint
2 cups orange juice
¾ cup lemon juice

- Bring water and sugar to boil until sugar dissolves. Remove from heat.
- Add tea bags and mint leaves. Steep tea for 6 to 8 minutes.
- Pour tea into gallon jug. Add orange juice and lemon juice.
- Add cold water to make one gallon.
- Note: Better if made 12 to 24 hours before serving.

Yields 1 gallon

Almond Tea

6 cups water
3 regular tea bags or 1 family-size tea bag
1 tablespoon almond extract
1 tablespoon vanilla extract
10 tablespoons fresh lemon juice or 7 tablespoons bottled lemon juice
½-1 cup sugar

- Boil 2 cups water, remove from heat. Add tea bags, extracts and lemon. Steep 10 minutes. Remove tea bags and discard.
- Boil remaining cups water; add sugar and boil for 4 minutes.
- Combine tea and sugar mixtures. Chill. Serve over ice.

Yields 6 cups

Orange Marmalade Tea

5 cups boiling water
1 family-size tea bag
½ cup orange marmalade
2 tablespoons sugar
2 tablespoons lemon juice

- Pour boiling water over tea bag; cover and steep five minutes.
- Remove tea bag, squeezing gently.
- Stir in marmalade, sugar and lemon juice.
- Strain mixture if desired.
- Serve hot or cold.

Yields 5 cups

Summer Fruit Tea

Refreshing on a hot summer day.

4½ tablespoons unsweetened
  instant tea
4 cups water
1½ cups sugar
1 (12 ounce) can frozen
  lemonade concentrate,
  thawed
1 (12 ounce) can frozen
  pineapple-orange juice
  concentrate, thawed
1 lemon, sliced for garnish
1 orange, sliced for garnish

- Mix tea, water and sugar.
- Bring to a boil; cool.
- Mix lemonade concentrate and pineapple-orange juice concentrate in a gallon container.
- Add tea and enough water to fill the container.
- Garnish with lemon and orange slices.

Serves 8 to 10

Spiced Cranberry Cider

1 (64 ounce) bottle apple cider
6 cups cranberry juice
⅓ cup firmly packed brown sugar
5 cinnamon sticks
1½ teaspoons whole cloves
1 lemon, thinly sliced

- Combine cider, cranberry juice and sugar in a large pan.
- Tie spices and lemon in a cheese cloth bag; drop into liquids.
- Bring to a boil then reduce heat and simmer 15 to 20 minutes.
- Serve hot.

Yields 28 servings

"It never fails, when I have a cocktail party, no matter where I put the food, my guests end up in the kitchen. People just feel at home in a kitchen…so I always put out a few bowls of nuts or other snacks in there as well."

Coffee Orleans

Makes a good after dinner drink!

6 cups dark-roasted coffee,
   brewed
6 ounces Kahlúa
6 tablespoons cocoa
Whipped cream for topping
Ground cinnamon for topping

- Brew coffee in coffee maker.
- Place 1 ounce Kahlúa and 1 tablespoon cocoa in each coffee cup. Pour coffee into each cup and add a dollop of whipped cream.
- Sprinkle with a dash of cinnamon if desired.

Serves 6

Coffee Punch

4 quarts strong, black coffee
1 quart whipping cream
6 tablespoons sugar
5 teaspoons vanilla
2 quarts vanilla ice cream

- Make coffee a day ahead and refrigerate until chilled.
- To serve, whip cream, adding sugar and vanilla.
- Spoon ice cream into a large punch bowl and add whipped cream mixture.
- Pour cold coffee over mixture and blend well.
- Serve in coffee cups.

Yields 50 cups

BREADS AND BRUNCHES
Stitch 'n Thyme

Stitch 'n Thyme

In 1985, the First Annual American Quilter's Society Show and Sale was held at the Executive Inn in Paducah, and the town hasn't been the same since. That year, quilters arrived by car, bus, and plane by the thousands, and were hard-pressed to find overnight lodging. Some found rooms in local motels; the rest were lucky to find lodging within a 50-mile radius. Undeterred by this inconvenience, quilters returned the following year in even larger numbers, and for the four days of the event, doubled the population of Paducah.

The influx of so many visitors would have been disastrous had it not been for Paducah hospitality. Local residents opened their hearts and their homes to quilt show attendees on a bed and breakfast basis. The hosts provided a room and daily continental breakfast for a nominal fee, which in many cases was donated to local civic organizations.

When we invite overnight guests into our homes, we cannot just offer coffee and doughnuts before we send them on their way. Bed and breakfast in many homes in Paducah means country ham, eggs, and biscuits in the morning, and a relaxing cup of tea or wine at the day's end.

Many quilt show guests find this arrangement to be superior to a room at a busy hotel or inn, and return to the same host homes year after year. Bonds of friendship have been formed, and guests and hosts remain in contact throughout the year.

During this busy week, area churches have discovered a profitable fundraiser. Ladies of the churches cook and serve luncheons or dinners that are attended and enjoyed by hundreds of quilters and locals alike. Paducahans have found these events to be great ways to enjoy delicious food and to mingle with quilters from all over the world.

Quilt Show week in Quilt City, U.S.A. is hospitality thyme.

Quilter's Brunch

Iced Mint Tea

Country Ham Quiche

Better than Gourmet Grits

Roasted Asparagus Parmesan

Scrumptious Coffee Cake

Seasonal Fresh Fruit

Stitch n' Thyme Ideas:

Quilting Be's:

Be organized. Great hospitality is in the details.
Be creative. Try spools of thread as place card holders.
Be humble. An accepted invitation is truly an honor for a host.

Eye of the Needle:

'Tis easier for guests to enter the doors of hospitality when hosts are gracious, accommodating, and having fun, too.

Jalapeño Cornbread

2 eggs
1 cup sour cream
1 (8 ounce) can cream style corn
1 jalapeño, seeded and finely
    chopped
1 cup grated cheddar cheese
1 cup yellow cornmeal
1 teaspoon baking soda
5 tablespoons butter, divided

- Preheat oven to 400°.
- In a mixing bowl, beat eggs lightly with whisk.
- Add sour cream, corn, jalapeño, cheddar cheese, corn-meal and baking soda. Mix all ingredients.
- Add 3 tablespoons of melted butter.
- In a 9 x 9-inch pan (greased) or 10-inch cast iron skillet, melt 2 tablespoons butter in oven.
- While pan is still hot, add batter and bake for 20 to 25 minutes.

Serves 8

Toasted English Muffin Bread

Delicious!

1 tablespoon butter
4 teaspoons cornmeal, divided
5½-6 cups bread flour, divided
2 packages dry yeast
1 tablespoon sugar
2 teaspoons salt
¼ teaspoon baking soda
2 cups milk
½ cup water

- Butter two, 8½ x 4½-inch pans and sprinkle each pan with 1 teaspoon cornmeal.
- Combine 3 cups flour, yeast, sugar, salt and baking soda, mixing well.
- Heat liquids until very warm (120° to 130°).
- Add to dry mixture and beat well.
- Stir in enough remaining flour to make a stiff batter.
- Spoon batter in pans and sprinkle tops with remaining cornmeal.
- Cover and let rise for 45 minutes.
- Preheat oven to 400°.
- Bake for 25 minutes.
- Remove bread from pans immediately and cool.
- Slice and toast to serve.

Yields 2 loaves

Lemon Poppy Seed Bread

½ cup margarine
1 cup sugar
2 eggs, slightly beaten
1½ cups flour
1 teaspoon baking powder
¼ teaspoon salt
½ cup milk
Grated rind of 1 lemon
2 teaspoons poppy seeds
1 cup confectioners' sugar, sifted
Juice of 1 lemon

- Preheat oven to 350°.
- Cream margarine with sugar. Add eggs and mix. Whisk together flour, baking powder and salt.
- Alternately add flour mixture and milk to margarine mixture, stirring constantly.
- Mix in grated lemon rind and poppy seeds. Bake in a greased 9 x 5-inch glass loaf pan for 50 to 60 minutes or until toothpick inserted in center comes out clean.
- Combine confectioners' sugar and juice to form topping. Pour over hot bread.
- Cool bread completely before slicing.

Yields 1 loaf

Bourbon Pecan Bread

3 cups flour
1 cup sugar
4 teaspoons baking powder
1½ teaspoons salt
¼ cup butter or margarine
1½ cups chopped pecans, divided
1 cup milk
½ cup bourbon
1 large egg

- Preheat oven to 350°.
- Combine flour, sugar, baking powder, and salt in a bowl.
- Cut in butter until mixture is crumbly.
- Add 1¼ cups pecans.
- Combine milk, bourbon and egg, stirring well. Add to dry ingredients, stirring just until moistened.
- Pour into a greased and floured 9 x 5-inch loaf pan. Sprinkle with remaining pecans.
- Bake for 50 to 60 minutes or until wooden toothpick inserted in center comes out clean.
- Cool in pan 10 minutes; remove from pan and cool completely on a wire rack.
- Note: This is for the bourbon lover.

Yields 1 loaf

Zucchini Bread

3 eggs

2 cups sugar

1 cup oil

2 cups peeled and shredded
    zucchini

3 teaspoons vanilla

3 cups flour

1 teaspoon salt

1 teaspoon baking soda

¼ teaspoon baking powder

3 teaspoons cinnamon

1 cup nuts

- Preheat oven to 350°.
- Beat eggs until light and foamy. Add sugar, oil, zucchini and vanilla.
- Combine flour, salt, baking soda, baking powder and cinnamon. Add to zucchini mixture.
- Stir until well blended; add nuts. Pour into two, greased 9 x 5 x 3-inch pans.
- Bake for 1 hour or until toothpick inserted in center comes out clean.
- Cool before serving.

Yields 2 loaves

Banana Chocolate Chip Bread

½ cup margarine or butter
1 cup sugar
2 eggs
¼ teaspoon salt
1 teaspoon vanilla
2 ripe bananas
1 teaspoon baking soda
2 cups flour
½ cup chopped pecans
½ cup mini chocolate chips

- Preheat oven to 350°.
- Cream butter and sugar in a large bowl.
- Add eggs, salt and vanilla mixing well.
- Mix in bananas.
- Combine baking soda and flour; add to creamed mixture.
- Stir in nuts and chocolate chips.
- Pour mixture into a greased 9 x 5-inch loaf pan.
- Bake for 50 minutes or until toothpick inserted in center comes out clean.

Serves 8 to 10

Cranberry Orange Muffins

A favorite on Thanksgiving and Christmas mornings!

½ cup chopped cranberries
5 tablespoons sugar, divided
2 teaspoons grated orange rind
1 cup flour
1 teaspoon baking powder
¼ teaspoon salt
1 egg, slightly beaten
¼ cup sour cream
¼ cup orange juice

- Preheat oven to 400°.
- Grease muffin tins.
- Mix cranberries, 2 tablespoons sugar and orange rind. Set aside.
- Sift flour, baking powder and salt into a bowl; add remaining sugar.
- Beat egg slightly, add sour cream and orange juice. Mix well.
- Fold into cranberry mixture.
- Spoon into muffin tins.
- Bake for 18 to 20 minutes or until golden brown.
- Cool before removing. Serve warm.

Serves 10

French Muffins

½ cup sugar
⅓ cup shortening
1 egg
1½ cups flour, sifted
1½ teaspoons baking powder, sifted
½ teaspoon salt
½ cup milk
¼ teaspoon nutmeg
1 teaspoon vanilla
¾ cup sugar
1¼ teaspoons cinnamon
½ cup butter, melted

- Preheat oven to 350°.
- Cream sugar, shortening and egg.
- Sift together flour, baking powder and salt. Add to cream mixture alternating with milk, beating well after each addition.
- Stir in nutmeg and vanilla.
- Fill greased muffin tins ⅔ full.
- Bake for 20 to 25 minutes.
- Combine sugar and cinnamon.
- While muffins are warm, dip into melted butter then roll in sugar and cinnamon.

Yield 12 muffins

Ginger Pear Muffins

2 cups flour
¾ cup firmly packed brown sugar
1 teaspoon baking soda
1 teaspoon salt
2 teaspoons ground ginger
1 teaspoon ground cinnamon
½ teaspoon ground cloves
1 cup plain yogurt
½ cup vegetable cooking oil
4 tablespoons molasses
1 egg
2 cups diced fresh pears
⅓ cup chopped walnuts

- Preheat oven to 350°.
- Mix flour, brown sugar, baking soda, salt, ginger, cinnamon and cloves in a large bowl.
- Mix yogurt, oil, molasses and egg in a separate bowl until well blended.
- Combine yogurt mixture to flour mixture; blend.
- Fold in pears and walnuts.
- Pour into muffin tins.
- Bake for 25 minutes.

Yields 18 muffins

Good Morning Muffins

A delicious way to start your day!

3 cups flour
1½ cups whole wheat flour
1½ cups raisin bran cereal
1 cup quick oats
1 cup chopped pecans
1 cup golden raisins
2½ cups packed brown sugar
1½ tablespoons baking soda
1½ tablespoons cinnamon
½ teaspoon salt
2 cups oil
6 eggs, beaten
1 cup grated carrots
1½ cups grated Granny Smith
   apples
2 tablespoons vanilla
½ cup sugar

- Preheat oven to 350°.
- Combine flours, cereal, oats, pecans, raisins and brown sugar.
- Add baking soda, cinnamon and salt. Mix well.
- Blend in oil and eggs.
- Fold in carrots, apples and vanilla.
- Grease muffin tins. Spoon mixture into muffin cups.
- Bake muffins for 15 minutes. Remove from oven. Sprinkle ½ teaspoon sugar on top of each muffin.
- Return to oven and bake an additional 15 to 20 minutes.
- Note: Batter will keep in refrigerator for up to one week.

Yields 36 to 48 muffins

Blackberry Scones

¼ cup butter
2 cups flour
¼ cup sugar
3½ teaspoons baking powder
¾ cup half-and-half
½ cup fresh or frozen blackberries
3 tablespoons sugar

- Preheat oven to 400°.
- Cut butter into flour until crumbly.
- Mix sugar with baking powder. Add to flour mixture.
- Add half-and-half, mixing well.
- Knead briefly; divide into two, 1-inch thick circles.
- Cut circles into quarters.
- Arrange blackberries on top of dough.
- Sprinkle evenly with sugar.
- Bake on an ungreased cookie sheet for 15 minutes.

Yields 8 scones

Cream Cheese Danish

2 (8 ounce) cans refrigerated
  crescent rolls
2 (8 ounce) packages cream
  cheese, softened
1 egg, separated
1 cup sugar
1 teaspoon vanilla
1 cup confectioners' sugar
1-2 tablespoons milk

- Preheat oven to 350°.
- Press 1 package crescent rolls in the bottom on an ungreased 9 x 13-inch cake pan.
- Beat together cream cheese, egg yolk, sugar, and vanilla until smooth. Spread over crescent rolls in pan.
- Press out remaining package of crescent rolls on lightly floured surface or waxed paper and seal perforations. Place on top of cream cheese, covering completely. Brush with egg white.
- Bake for 25 minutes or until top is golden brown.
- Remove from oven and immediately spread on paste made from confectioners' sugar and milk. This will melt to form a glaze.
- Note: This is better if made a day ahead and may be served warmed or cold.

Yields 20 Danishes

Cinnamon Cheese Blintzes

Serve at coffees or brunches.

1 cup sugar, divided
4 tablespoons cinnamon
2 loaves thinly sliced white
  bread, crusts removed
2 (8 ounce) package cream
  cheese, softened
2 egg yolks
1 cup butter, melted

- Preheat oven to 350°.
- Mix ½ cup sugar and cinnamon in a bowl.
- Roll bread with a rolling pin.
- Mix cream cheese, egg yolks, and ½ cup sugar.
- Spread cream cheese mixture on bread slices, then roll up in pinwheels.
- Dip into melted butter and roll into sugar and cinnamon mixture.
- Place on a cookie sheet. Slice each roll in 3 pieces.
- Bake for 8 minutes.
- Note: These freeze well in freezer bags. Bake for 8 minutes if rolls are thawed or 10 to 12 minutes if frozen.

Yields 100 rolls

Mini Southern Buttermilk Biscuits

These are nice for cocktail parties, breakfast, or family dinners!

1 cup flour, sifted
1 teaspoon baking powder
⅛ teaspoon baking soda
¼ teaspoon salt
2 tablespoons unsalted butter
⅓ cup buttermilk

- Preheat oven to 350°. Line baking sheet with wax paper.
- Combine flour, baking powder, baking soda, and salt. Blend thoroughly.
- Cream in the butter with fork until mixture is coarse.
- Add buttermilk slowly and mix with a fork until smooth.
- On a floured surface, roll out dough with a rolling pin until ½-inch thick (flour rolling pin if necessary).
- Use a shot glass for mini-biscuits or for larger biscuits, use a glass to press out biscuits.
- Place rounds on baking sheet and bake until golden on top; approximately 12 to 17 minutes. Watch carefully not to burn.

Variations: Add a teaspoon of dill or rosemary to ingredients and serve with beef or pork!

Yields 16 mini biscuits

Parmesan Poppy Seed Popovers

¼ cup freshly grated Parmesan
*   cheese*
1 cup milk
1 cup flour
1 tablespoon butter, melted
¼ teaspoon salt
2 large eggs
1 teaspoon poppy seeds

- Place oven rack on next to lowest shelf. Preheat oven to 450°.
- Grease 6 deep muffin or popover pans. Sprinkle with Parmesan and set aside.
- Combine milk, flour, butter and salt.
- Beat eggs slightly. Add eggs and poppy seeds to flour mixture and beat until just blended. Overbeating the batter will reduce the volume of popovers.
- Fill cups ¾ full.
- Bake for 15 minutes. Reduce heat to 350° (do not open oven door) and bake an additional 20 minutes.
- Remove popovers with a spatula and serve immediately.

Yields 6 popovers

Sour Cream Dinner Rolls

1 (8 ounce) container sour
   cream
½ cup butter
½ cup sugar
1¼ teaspoons salt
2 packages dry yeast
½ cup warm water
2 large eggs
4 cups flour
2 tablespoons butter, melted

- Combine sour cream, butter, sugar and salt in a sauce-pan and cook on medium heat. Stir occasionally. Cool.
- Dissolve yeast in warm water in a glass measuring cup. Let stand 5 minutes.
- Stir yeast mixture, eggs, sour cream mixture and flour together in a large bowl until well blended.
- Cover and chill for 8 hours.
- Divide dough into fourths and shape each into a ball. Roll each ball into a ¼-inch thickness on a floured surface.
- Cut dough with a small, round cutter or a small-rimmed cup. Brush the rounds with melted butter.
- Make a crease with a knife and fold in half and seal edges gently.
- Place rolls on a jelly-roll pan close together.
- Cover and let rise 45 minutes or until doubled. Keep free from drafts!
- Bake at 375° for 12 to 15 minutes.

Yields approximately 4 dozen rolls

"One of our most memorable tailgating parties happened right in our own driveway! We parked the truck, pulled the tailgate down, and friends and neighbors joined in the school spirit."

Savory Yeast Rolls

1 (¼ ounce) package dry yeast

2 cups warm water (105° to 115°)

6 cups flour

½ cup sugar

½ teaspoon salt

½ cup butter-flavored shortening

2 large eggs, lightly beaten

½ cup butter, melted

- Dissolve yeast in warm water in a small bowl. Let stand 5 minutes.
- Sift together flour, sugar and salt in a large bowl.
- Cut shortening into flour mixture until crumbly. Stir in yeast and eggs until just blended.
- Cover and chill for 8 to 36 hours.
- Roll dough to ¼-inch thickness on a well-floured surface (dough will be soft). Cut with a 3-inch round cutter or a glass cup.
- Brush rounds with butter. Make a crease across each round with a knife and fold in half, gently press edges to seal.
- Place rolls on a 15 x 10-inch jelly-roll pan or cookie sheet.
- Cover and let rise in a warm, draft-free area for 45 minutes or until doubled in size.
- Preheat oven to 400°.
- Bake for 8 to 10 minutes or until golden brown.

Yields 3 dozen rolls

Not for Tea-Thyme Scones

These scones offer a tasty twist to the traditional but slightly sweet version.

¼ cup butter, melted

½ cup milk

2 tablespoons sugar

½ cup yellow cornmeal

1½ cups flour

¼ teaspoon salt

1 teaspoon baking powder

2 tablespoons chopped fresh
   thyme leaves (or 1 tablespoon
   dried)

- Preheat oven to 375°.
- Lightly coat a baking sheet with nonstick spray.
- Combine butter and milk in a measuring cup.
- Sift together sugar, cornmeal, flour, salt and baking powder in a mixing bowl.
- Add the milk mixture to the dry ingredients and stir until blended.
- Stir in thyme leaves.
- Place dough on a floured board and shape into a round ½-inch thick.
- Cut into 6 wedges.
- Place wedges on baking sheet and bake for 15 to 20 minutes or until golden brown.
- Serve warm.
- Note: These freeze well.

Yields 6 scones

Italian Bread

2 packages dry yeast

1 teaspoon sugar

6 cups lukewarm water

6 pounds flour*

6 teaspoons salt

½ cup butter, melted

- Dissolve yeast and sugar in water.
- Pour flour into a large pan. Add salt, butter and yeast mixture. Mix well.
- Flour surface and knead dough until smooth.
- Cover and let rise for 1 hour.
- Knead dough again and form into 6 loaves. Let rise another hour.
- Preheat oven to 350°.
- Grease and flour cookie sheet. Bake bread for 1 hour.

Yields 6 loaves

*1 pound of flour equals 3½ cups.

Rosemary and Black Olive Focaccia

2 tablespoons yellow cornmeal

½ cup warm water (105° to 115°)

1 tablespoon sugar

1 package dry yeast

3-4 cups bread flour, divided

½ teaspoon salt

⅓ cup plus 3 tablespoons olive oil, divided

3 tablespoons chopped fresh rosemary

⅓ cup pitted and chopped kalamata olives

- Sprinkle a 12-inch pizza pan or baking sheet with cornmeal.
- Combine water, sugar and yeast in a measuring cup. Let stand for 2 to 3 minutes, until foamy.
- Sift together 3 cups of flour and salt.
- Add yeast mixture, ⅓ cup olive oil, rosemary and olives. Beat until well blended. Add more flour as needed until dough is smooth and elastic.
- Roll dough into a 12-inch round and place on baking pan.
- Let rise in a warm place until doubled (about 45 minutes).
- Preheat oven to 400°.
- Make indentations with your fingers all over the dough.
- Drizzle with remaining olive oil.
- Bake 20 to 25 minutes or until golden brown.
- Remove from baking pan and cool on a wire rack.
- Note: Serve as a complement to a favorite pasta dish or use to make delicious, different sandwiches.

Serves 4 to 6

"Love is sweet, but it's nice to have bread with it."
Yiddish wisdom

Country Ham Quiche

1 unbaked 9-inch pie shell

4 eggs, beaten

1 cup half-and-half

1 cup shredded country ham, cooked

½ cup shredded cheddar cheese

½ cup shredded mozzarella cheese

1 teaspoon cracked black pepper

⅛ teaspoon cayenne pepper

- Preheat oven to 350°.
- Grease quiche dish and line with pie shell.
- Beat eggs well; whisk in half-and-half.
- Mix remaining ingredients and combine with liquid mixture.
- Pour into pie shell.
- Bake uncovered for 45 to 50 minutes or until knife inserted in the center comes out clean.
- Note: If edges are browning too quickly, cover with foil.

Serves 6

Italian Sausage Quiche

Excellent for a luncheon with friends!

1 unbaked 9-inch pie shell

1 pound Italian sausage, crumbled

1 pound fresh mushrooms, sliced

2 cups shredded Swiss cheese

4 eggs, beaten

1 cup whipping cream

¼ teaspoon salt

- Preheat oven to 425°.
- Line quiche dish with pie shell.
- Prick bottom and sides with a fork.
- Bake crust for 6 to 8 minutes. Let cool.
- Decrease oven temperature to 350°.
- Cook sausage until browned; drain. Reserve 2 tablespoons drippings.
- Saute mushrooms in reserved drippings; drain.
- Combine sausage, mushrooms, cheese, eggs, cream and salt. Mix well.
- Pour into pie shell and bake for 45 minutes or until set.

Serves 8

Sunday Morning Quiche

Serve this for Christmas brunch with Roasted Asparagus Parmesan (page 149).

1 unbaked 9-inch pie shell
1 yellow onion, chopped
½ green bell pepper, chopped
4 large eggs
1 cup half-and-half
1 cup shredded cheddar cheese
1 cup shredded mozzarella cheese
1 cup shredded provolone cheese
3 green onions, chopped
¼ teaspoon cayenne pepper
Salt and pepper to taste

- Preheat oven to 350°.
- Grease quiche dish and line with pie shell.
- Mix all ingredients in a large bowl.
- Pour into pie shell.
- Bake for 45 to 50 minutes or until knife inserted in the center comes out clean.
- Slice and serve warm.

Serves 6

Turkey-Asparagus Brunch Bake

1 pound fresh asparagus
1 pound ground turkey
1 cup chopped onion
½ cup chopped sweet red pepper
3 eggs
2 cups whole milk
1 cup flour
¼ cup grated Parmesan cheese
1 teaspoon lemon-pepper
   seasoning
1 teaspoon dried tarragon, basil
   or thyme, crushed
1 cup shredded Swiss cheese

- Preheat oven to 425°.
- Wash asparagus and cut into 1½-inch pieces.
- Cook asparagus in a small amount of boiling water for 4 to 8 minutes or until crisp and tender.
- In a large skillet, cook turkey, onion and red peppers until vegetables are just tender and turkey is cooked through. Remove from heat and drain. Set aside.
- Grease a 3-quart rectangular baking dish. Arrange meat mixture in dish; top with asparagus.
- Combine eggs, milk, flour, Parmesan cheese, lemon-pepper seasoning and tarragon; beat until smooth. Pour egg mixture evenly over casserole.
- Bake for 20 minutes or until knife inserted in the middle of the casserole comes out clean.
- Sprinkle with Swiss cheese and bake 3 to 5 additional minutes.
- Note: May be prepared ahead and refrigerated until baking time. Increase cook time to 30 minutes if refrigerated.

Serves 6 to 8

Layered Breakfast Casserole

Great for a weekend brunch with neighbors.

1 (12 ounce) can evaporated
   milk
3 slices bacon, diced
¼ pound chipped beef, cut
   julienne
4 tablespoons butter, divided
¾ cup mushrooms, sliced
¼ cup flour
8 eggs
¾ teaspoon salt
Pepper to taste

- Preheat oven to 275°.
- Pour ½ cup of evaporated milk into a bowl. Set aside.
- Add water to remaining milk to make 2 cups.
- Fry bacon until crisp; remove grease from frying pan.
- Combine bacon, chipped beef, 2 tablespoons butter and mushrooms in a frying pan.
- Sprinkle flour over mixture and gradually add evaporated milk and water mixture.
- Cook and stir until mixture thickens.
- Season with salt and pepper; set aside.
- Melt remaining 2 tablespoons butter. Add eggs, salt, and reserved evaporated milk.
- Scramble in a large skillet, keeping eggs moist.
- In an 8 x 8-inch glass dish, alternate layers of eggs and sauce.
- Bake for 45 minutes or until thoroughly heated.
- Note: May be prepared one day ahead and refrigerated. Remove from refrigerator 30 minutes prior to baking.

Serves 6

> *"My china is basic white with silver trim. To add a little extra to the table, I tie a fresh flower or herb to the stem of the wineglass with a pretty ribbon. This works well with napkin rings, too."*

Canadian Bacon and Egg Casserole

Canadian bacon makes this a real hit!

6 tablespoons butter, divided
2 tablespoons flour
½ teaspoon salt
½ teaspoon pepper
3 cups milk
1 cup shredded cheddar cheese
1 cup chopped Canadian bacon
½ cup chopped onion
12 eggs, beaten
2 (2.5 ounce) cans sliced
*   mushrooms*
2 tablespoons butter
1 cup bread crumbs
⅛ teaspoon paprika

- Preheat oven to 350°.
- In a saucepan, combine 3 tablespoons melted butter, flour, salt and pepper. Gradually add milk. Cook over medium heat, stirring constantly.
- Add cheese, stirring until melted. Set aside.
- Saute the Canadian bacon and onion in remaining butter.
- Add eggs and cook until scrambled.
- Fold in drained mushrooms and cheese sauce.
- Spoon mixture into a lightly greased 12 x 7 x 2-inch pan.
- Melt butter and pour over bread crumbs; toss.
- Top casserole with bread crumbs and paprika.
- Bake for 30 minutes.
- Note: May be made ahead the night before and refrigerated. Remove 30 minutes before baking.

Serves 8

"Sunday brunch means family at our house. And I mean the WHOLE family! It's our most relaxing time of the week so it was only natural that we made it a special time for family entertaining. A practical tip for family 'brunching' — prepare some foods the evening before, so you're not pressed for time early that morning."

Better Than Gourmet Grits

Great for brunch or with grilled pork!

2 cups water
2 cups half-and-half
1 cup grits
½ cup butter
2 eggs, beaten
2 cups cheddar cheese, shredded
3 tablespoons minced garlic
1 teaspoon pepper
1 teaspoon salt
¼ teaspoon cayenne pepper
2 teaspoons hot sauce

- Boil water and half-and-half in a large saucepan.
- Add grits.
- Reduce heat to medium. Cover and cook approximately 20 minutes.
- Preheat oven to 350°.
- Add remaining ingredients to cooked grits and mix well.
- Pour grits into a greased 2-quart casserole dish.
- Top with extra cheese, if desired.
- Cover and bake for 1 hour.
- Serve hot.

Serves 6

Green Chile Brunch Casserole

A delicious way to serve eggs with a kick.

6 (4 ounce) cans whole green chiles
10 eggs
3 tablespoons flour
1 (16 ounce) container sour cream
1 cup shredded Monterey Jack cheese
1½ cups shredded long horn cheese

- Preheat oven to 350°.
- Drain chiles and slice open. (Optional: remove seeds for milder taste.)
- Prepare 9 x 13-inch dish with cooking spray.
- Combine eggs, flour and sour cream in blender. Mix well and reserve.
- Mix cheeses. Layer the dish with chiles then cheese and repeat.
- Poke holes into the layers.
- Pour egg mixture over casserole.
- Bake for 45 minutes.
- Cool 15 minutes before serving.

Serves 6 to 8

Caramel Cinnamon Strata

Great for an elegant brunch yet easy enough to serve anytime!

¾ cup firmly packed dark brown
 sugar
6 tablespoons butter
1 tablespoon light corn syrup
1 teaspoon cinnamon
12 slices white sandwich bread,
 crusts removed
6 large eggs
1½ cups whole milk
1 teaspoon vanilla
¼ teaspoon salt
Strawberries for garnish
Kiwi for garnish

- Combine brown sugar, butter, corn syrup and cinnamon in a heavy saucepan. Cook over low heat, stirring until sugar dissolves.
- Bring to a boil and remove from heat.
- Pour into a 9 x 13-inch glass dish. Spread to cover entire dish.
- Allow mixture to cool.
- Arrange six slices of bread on top of caramel mixture. Add second layer of bread slices.
- Whisk eggs, milk, vanilla and salt together. Pour over bread.
- Cover and chill overnight.
- Preheat oven to 350°.
- Bake uncovered for 40 minutes or until bread is golden brown.
- Remove from oven and let stand for 5 minutes.
- Cut into 6 servings and invert on plates.
- Garnish with strawberries and kiwi. Serve immediately.

Serves 8

Buttermilk Coffee Cake

½ cup margarine, softened
2 cups firmly packed brown
 sugar
2 cups flour
1 egg
1 teaspoon baking soda
½ teaspoon salt
½ teaspoon cinnamon
1 cup buttermilk
2 teaspoons vanilla
1½ cups chopped pecans

- Preheat oven to 350°.
- Mix margarine, brown sugar and flour. Reserve 1 cup; set aside.
- Add all remaining ingredients except pecans.
- Pour into a greased 9 x 13-inch pan.
- Sprinkle with reserved ingredients and pecans.
- Bake for 25 minutes or until a toothpick inserted in the center comes out clean.

Yields 16 squares

Scrumptious Coffee Cake

Great dish for a brunch with friends!

1 cup butter, softened

1 cup sugar

2 eggs

2 cups self-rising flour

1 (8 ounce) container sour
  cream

½ teaspoon almond or vanilla
  extract

1 can whole berry cranberry
  sauce

½ cup chopped pecans

Glaze:

1 cup powdered sugar, sifted

2 tablespoons milk

½ teaspoon vanilla extract

- Preheat oven to 350°.
- Cream butter. Gradually add sugar and mix on medium speed.
- Add eggs one at a time, beating after each addition.
- Add flour and sour cream alternately.
- Stir in almond or vanilla extract.
- Pour batter in a greased 9 x 13-inch glass dish.
- Carefully spread cranberry sauce over batter and top with nuts.
- Bake for 35 to 40 minutes or until a knife inserted in the center comes out clean.
- To make glaze, mix powdered sugar, milk and vanilla extract.
- Drizzle glaze over hot cake.

Serves 10

"Think about the colors on the plate when selecting your menu. Presentation is 50% of the pleasure of eating."

German Apple Pancakes

4 eggs
¾ cup flour
¾ cup milk
½ teaspoon salt
¼ cup margarine, divided
2 medium thinly sliced Granny
    Smith apples
¼ cup sugar
¼ teaspoon ground cinnamon

- Preheat oven to 400°.
- Place two 8-inch round pans in oven.
- Beat eggs, flour, milk and salt on medium speed for 1 minute.
- Remove pans from oven and place 2 tablespoons margarine in each pan, coating sides.
- Divide apple slices and arrange in each pan.
- Pour equal amounts of batter over apples.
- Bake uncovered for 20 to 25 minutes or until puffed and golden brown.
- Serve immediately with maple syrup.
- Note: The pancakes will fall like a soufflé.

Serves 4

Overnight Sticky Pecan Ring

Perfect for Sunday mornings.

1 (18 count) frozen Parker
    House style roll dough
1 (4 serving) package vanilla
    pudding mix (do not use
    instant)
½ cup firmly packed brown
    sugar
½ cup chopped pecans
½ cup butter, melted

- Separate frozen roll dough into pieces.
- Combine dry pudding mix with brown sugar and pecans.
- Place pieces of roll dough in a well-buttered Bundt pan.
- Pour melted butter oven frozen dough.
- Sprinkle with pudding mixture.
- Cover cake pan with a towel and let sit overnight. (The dough will rise by morning.)
- Preheat oven to 350°.
- Bake for 20 minutes.
- Invert on a serving platter.
- Pull apart to eat.

Serves 10 to 12

Sweet and Savory French Toast

Perfect for Saturday mornings.

4 ounces cream cheese
8 slices raisin bread
1 apple, peeled and chopped
1 banana, peeled and chopped
2 eggs, beaten
¼ cup milk
½ tablespoon cinnamon
Confectioners' sugar for garnish

- Spread cream cheese on bread slices.
- Put 1 tablespoon of apples and bananas on 4 slices of bread.
- Top with remaining bread slices.
- Mix egg, milk and cinnamon in a bowl. Dip "sandwiches" into egg mixture and cook on a lightly greased griddle or skillet until browned on both sides.
- Sprinkle with confectioners' sugar. Serve with syrup.

Serves 4

"Be careful lest we be entertaining angels unaware…"

Hebrews 13:2

Soups and Salads

Springthyme

Springthyme

Spring can never arrive soon enough in Paducah. After the bleak, cold days of winter, the emergence of spring bulbs—tulips, hyacinths, and jonquils—is a joyous sight. A few weeks later, dogwood trees and azaleas show their radiant blossoms. The display is so beautiful that it calls for a celebration—Dogwood Festival.

Conceived by the Civic Beautification Board, the festival began on a modest scale, with area garden clubs going door to door through neighborhoods, asking residents to illuminate their dogwood trees at night. In the beginning, only a few areas participated, but as interest grew, more neighborhoods became involved. Today, the trail of lighted dogwoods extends from the city hall downtown to historic Lower Town, the stately homes of Jefferson Street, and to several sections of Paducah's west end. So that all may enjoy the pageantry, city buses transport people from City Hall to the trail's end.

And what has this to do with entertaining? Dogwood thyme is the perfect time to rejoin friends and neighbors after hibernating for the winter. Hosting a festive spring luncheon is a favorite way to entertain family and good friends or even visitors who have come to view the magnificent dogwoods. Lunching outdoors overlooking a well tended Western Kentucky garden provides added enjoyment. The fare is light and always delicious, featuring picture-perfect salads or chilled soups and not-too-sinful desserts.

In Paducah, spring is the thyme to celebrate the beauty of the dogwood trees with festive food.

Dogwood Festival Luncheon

Almond Tea

Gazpacho with Gusto

Confetti Chicken Salad
with Lime Vinaigrette

Savory Yeast Rolls

Old Fashioned Strawberry Pie

Springthyme Tips:

Spring Forward:
It's never too early to plan for next year's event. Check your local community calendars for dates and times.

Birds and the Bees:
Protect your guests and food from outdoor pests with citronella candles or sprays.

Tortilla Soup

3 tablespoons corn oil

4 corn tortillas, cut into long
1-inch strips

6 cloves garlic, peeled and
coarsely chopped

1 large onion, diced and puréed
until almost smooth

4 cups tomato purée

1 jalapeño, seeded and minced

1 tablespoon cumin

1 large bay leaf

4-5 cups chicken stock or broth

Salt to taste

Juice of ½ lemon

Cayenne pepper to taste

2 chicken breasts, cooked and
shredded

⅔ cup frozen corn

Garnishes:
Grated cheddar cheese
Avocado, cubed
Tortilla chips, crumbled
Sour cream

- Heat oil in a large soup pot over medium heat.
- Add tortilla strips and garlic. Sauté until tortillas are crisp, about 4 to 5 minutes.
- Add onion purée and cook for 3 minutes stirring occasionally.
- Add tomato purée, jalapeño, cumin, bay leaf and chicken stock. Bring to a boil.
- Lower heat and simmer for 30 minutes. If soup becomes too thick, thin out with additional chicken stock.
- Season to taste with salt, lemon juice and cayenne pepper.
- Add chicken and corn then simmer another 30 minutes.
- Serve with garnishes.

Serves 4

"Instead of buying fresh cut flowers for your centerpiece, use a large basket and add 3" or 4" pots of annuals, greenery and perennials until full. After the party, plant them in your yard or garden."

Loaded Potato Soup

4 large russet potatoes
1 stalk celery, finely minced
1 small onion, finely minced
1 carrot, grated
4 cups chicken broth
2 teaspoons salt
1 tablespoon white vinegar
3 cups milk
½ cup flour
1 cup shredded cheddar cheese
1 cup shredded Monterey Jack
  cheese

Garnishes:
Sour cream
Cheddar cheese
Bacon
Green onion

- Peel potatoes and chop into bite-size pieces.
- Combine potatoes, celery, onion and carrot with chicken broth, salt and vinegar in a Dutch oven over medium heat. Bring to a boil, then reduce heat and simmer for 20 minutes.
- In a separate bowl, whisk together milk and flour.
- Remove from heat and add milk and flour mixture.
- Return to heat and simmer 10 minutes or until thickened, stirring occasionally.
- Add cheeses and continue to cook until desired thickness.
- Garnish with sour cream, cheddar cheese, bacon and green onion.

Serves 6

Slow Cooked Onion Soup

1 tablespoon olive oil
1 teaspoon dried rosemary
3 large onions, coarsely chopped
¼ teaspoon salt, divided
Cracked pepper
½ cup dry red wine
3 cups water
1 pound mushrooms, coarsely
  chopped
2 medium carrots, diced
½ cup finely chopped pecans,
  toasted
1 large tomato, diced
2 cups chopped fresh basil leaves

- Heat olive oil over medium heat in a large stock pot.
- Stir in rosemary, onions, ⅛ teaspoon salt and a few grinds of pepper.
- Reduce heat to low and sauté stirring frequently for 30 minutes. Onions should be very soft and nearly browned.
- Stir in wine slowly, then add water, mushrooms, carrots and remaining salt. Increase heat to high and bring to a gentle boil.
- Reduce heat to low and simmer 15 minutes.
- Add pecans, tomato and basil to soup. Cook 5 minutes longer. Serve hot.

Serves 8 to 10

Winter White Chili

2½ cups water

2 teaspoons lemon-pepper
 seasoning

2 teaspoons cumin seed

4 boneless, skinless chicken
 breasts, cut into 1-inch cubes

1 teaspoon olive oil or nonstick
 cooking spray

1 garlic clove, minced

1 cup chopped onions

2 (9 ounce) packages frozen
 shoe-peg white corn, thawed

2 (4.5 ounce) cans chopped
 green chiles, undrained

2 teaspoons cumin

3 tablespoons fresh lime juice

2 (15.5 ounce) cans great
 northern white beans

Optional Toppings:

1 cup crushed tortilla chips

1 cup shredded Parmesan cheese

1 (16 ounce) jar salsa verde

1 (16 ounce) container sour
 cream

- In medium stock pot, combine water, lemon-pepper seasoning and cumin seed. Bring to a boil.
- Add chicken and reduce heat to low; simmer for 20 minutes or until chicken is tender.
- Spray medium skillet with nonstick cooking spray. Over medium heat, add garlic and cook for 1 minute. Remove garlic and add to chicken mixture.
- Cook onions in skillet until tender.
- Remove onions and add to chicken mixture along with corn, chiles, cumin and lime juice. Bring to a boil.
- Add beans. Reduce heat to low and simmer for 30 minutes.
- Top with crushed tortilla chips, cheese or a tablespoon of salsa verde or sour cream. A great complement for this chili is warm Jalapeño Cornbread on page 44. Spice up this recipe with more cumin and/or chopped jalapeños!

Serves 8

"The beauty of the house is order. The blessing of the house is contentment; the glory of the house is hospitality."

A House Blessing

French Onion Soup Au Gratin

4 tablespoons butter

3 large yellow onions, thinly sliced

¼ cup sugar

¼ teaspoon salt

½ teaspoon pepper

2 cloves garlic, chopped

6 cups beef stock or canned beef broth

4 large slices French bread, thickly sliced and lightly toasted

1 cup grated Gruyère cheese or 4 thin slices of Swiss cheese

- Melt butter in soup pot over medium-low heat.
- Add onions and sauté for 5 minutes. Reduce heat to low. Cover and cook for 20 to 25 minutes, stirring often.
- Sprinkle sugar over onions, tossing well to coat. Cook uncovered for 10 minutes to caramelize, stirring often.
- Season with salt and pepper. Add garlic and stir well. Cook for 2 minutes.
- Slowly add beef stock, blending well and increasing heat to bring to a boil. Reduce heat and allow soup to simmer for 30 minutes uncovered.
- Divided soup into 4 oven-proof bowls. Top each with a toasted slice of French bread and sprinkle with cheese evenly on top.
- Place soup bowls on a baking sheet and under a broiler. Broil until cheese melts and browns slightly.

Serves 4

Spinach Tortellini Soup

6 cups low sodium chicken broth

1 (9 ounce) package cheese tortellini

½ (10 ounce) package fresh spinach, slightly chopped

6 teaspoons minced garlic

1 teaspoon dried basil

Salt and pepper to taste

1 (14.5 ounce) can Italian-style diced tomatoes

- In a large soup pot, bring chicken broth to a simmer.
- Stir in tortellini and simmer gently for 3 minutes.
- Stir in spinach, garlic, basil, salt, pepper and tomatoes. Return to a simmer for 2 to 3 more minutes.
- Serve hot with crusty bread.
- Note: Doubles nicely.

Serves 4

Chicken Barley Soup

2-3 pounds chicken breasts
1 medium carrot, sliced
1-2 stalks of celery, sliced
1 bay leaf
½ cup uncooked barley
2 teaspoons salt
2 teaspoons instant chicken
 bouillon
2 cups water
2 cans chicken broth
½ teaspoon pepper
1½ cups chopped leeks

- Place chicken breasts, carrots, celery, bay leaf, barley, salt, chicken bouillon, water, chicken broth and pepper in a large Dutch oven.
- Heat until boiling. Reduce heat to simmer. Cook for 30 minutes.
- Remove chicken from stock.
- Cut up chicken into small pieces and return to soup.
- Add leeks and heat to boiling. Reduce heat again to low and simmer for 30 more minutes.
- Remove bay leaf before serving.
- Note: More chicken or vegetables may be added depending upon how hearty you like your soup.

Serves 6

Hot Cucumber Soup

Great for a winter night with friends!

2 tablespoons real butter
1 medium yellow onion, chopped
3½ cups chicken stock
1 small potato, peeled and
 chopped
3 cucumbers, peeled, seeded and
 diced
½ cup sour cream or heavy
 cream
Salt and pepper to taste
2 tablespoons fresh dill or basil
 for garnish

- Over medium heat, melt butter. Add onion and sauté until tender.
- Add the chicken stock and potato. Bring to a boil. Reduce heat and simmer for 10 minutes uncovered.
- Add cucumbers. Continue to simmer until cucumbers are soft.
- Add cream, salt and pepper. Cook until heated.
- Pour into food processor or blender and purée until smooth. If too thick, add more stock or water.
- Place in a large bowl and cover. Refrigerate overnight. Reheat and serve with garnish!

Variation: May use 1 cup plain yogurt in place of cream and serve cold!

Serves 6

Spicy Shrimp and Corn Soup

1 cup oil
1 cup flour
3 cups whole kernel corn, fresh
    or canned
1 large yellow onion, chopped
1 large bell pepper, chopped
4 stalks celery, chopped
3 tablespoons minced garlic
2 cups diced fresh tomatoes
1 (8 ounce) can tomato sauce
3 whole bay leaves
1 teaspoon dried thyme
1 teaspoon dried basil
3 quarts water
4½ dozen shrimp, uncooked,
    peeled and deveined
1 bunch green onions, chopped
1 cup chopped fresh parsley
1 teaspoon hot sauce
1 tablespoon Creole seasoning
Salt and pepper to taste

- In a large stockpot, heat oil over medium heat. Add flour slowly. Use a wire whisk or wooden spoon to constantly stir until roux is golden brown. Be very careful not to burn.
- Add corn, onion, bell pepper, celery, garlic and tomatoes. Sauté about 10 minutes.
- Add tomato sauce, bay leaves, thyme, basil and water slowly. Stir constantly.
- Bring to a small boil, then reduce heat to simmer for approximately 30 minutes.
- Add shrimp, green onions, parsley and remaining seasonings. Cook 10 to 15 minutes.
- Serve with hot French Bread.

Serves 10

Curried Pumpkin Soup

A delicious way to warm up a chilly autumn day.

1 cup chopped onion
1 garlic clove
¼ cup butter
1 teaspoon curry powder
½ teaspoon salt
¼ teaspoon coriander
⅛ teaspoon crushed red pepper
3 cups chicken broth
1¾ cups solid packed pumpkin
1 cup half-and-half
Sour cream for garnish
Chives for garnish

- Sauté onion and garlic in butter until soft. Add curry powder, salt, coriander and pepper. Cook 1 minute.
- Add chicken broth, cook 15 to 20 minutes.
- Add pumpkin and half-and-half. Cook an additional 5 minutes.
- Garnish with sour cream and chives.
- Note: For a smoother consistency, put soup in food processor and purée.

Serves 6 to 8

Roasted Garlic, Butternut Squash and Granny Smith Apple Soup

40 cloves garlic, unpeeled (about 2 heads)

1 tablespoon olive oil

1 (2 pound) butternut squash

2 large Granny Smith apples

1 medium onion

6 cups chicken or vegetable broth

2 tablespoons sugar

¼-½ teaspoon dried rosemary, crushed

¼ cup dry sherry

Salt to taste

Ground black pepper to taste

1 cup heavy cream (optional)

- Preheat oven to 325°.
- Toss unpeeled garlic cloves with olive oil. Spread in a single layer on a baking sheet. Bake until garlic collapses and is golden brown, about 15 minutes. When cool enough to handle, squeeze the pulp from the cloves into a glass bowl. Set aside. (This can be done several days in advance. Cover and refrigerate roasted garlic.)
- Peel, seed and coarsely chop squash.
- Peel, core and coarsely chop apples.
- Slice onion.
- Put the squash, apples and onion into a 4-quart soup pot.
- Add six cups chicken/vegetable broth. Add more broth or water if necessary to cover vegetables.
- Stir in sugar, roasted garlic and rosemary. Bring to a boil and simmer uncovered until the vegetables and apples are soft; about 30 to 40 minutes.
- Remove solids with a slotted spoon and purée them in batches in a food processor or food mill. Purée liquid in batches if necessary.
- Return puréed mixtures to pot, stir and bring to a boil. It should have a velvety thickness. If soup is too thin, cook uncovered over medium heat to reduce and thicken. If too thick, stir in a little more broth.
- Stir in sherry, salt and pepper. Add cream and heat thoroughly, but do not allow the soup to boil.
- Note: This is a low-fat dish and do not be afraid to use too much garlic; it will become very mellow and will not overpower the squash or apples.

Yields 10 cups

Gazpacho with Gusto

1 cup chopped onion
3 cucumbers, peeled, seeded and
    chopped
2 green peppers, chopped
6 cups canned tomatoes
2 cups consommé
½ cup lemon juice
1½ cups vegetable juice
1 cup spicy vegetable juice
½ cup olive oil
2½ teaspoons salt
¼ teaspoon pepper
½ teaspoon tarragon
½ teaspoon basil
¼ teaspoon marjoram
¼ teaspoon oregano
½ teaspoon parsley
3 garlic cloves, minced
Croutons for topping
Sour cream for topping

- Combine all ingredients in a large bowl.
- Put two cups at a time in food processor and blend until pourable but slightly chunky.
- Chill.
- Top with croutons and a dollop of sour cream.

Makes 4 quarts

Chilled Raspberry Soup

Serve for a ladies' luncheon.

2 (12 ounce) packages frozen
    raspberries, thawed
½ cup sour cream
⅓ cup sugar
2 cups ice water
½ cup red wine
Whipped cream for garnish
Fresh strawberries and
    raspberries for garnish

- In a blender, purée raspberries until smooth.
- Add sour cream and sugar and blend well on medium-low speed.
- Add ice water and wine; blend again.
- Pour and press mixture twice through a mesh strainer to remove seeds.
- Cover and chill overnight.
- Shake soup before serving.
- For a pretty presentation, serve in wine goblets.
- Garnish with a dollop of whipped cream and fresh berries. Serve cold.

Serves 6 to 8

Summerthyme Salad

4 boneless, skinless chicken breasts

1 tablespoon olive oil

Salt and pepper

Thyme Vinaigrette

½ pound mixed salad greens

4 ounces crumbled blue cheese, divided

1 orange, peeled and thinly sliced

1 Vidalia or sweet onion, peeled and thinly sliced

1½ cups fresh strawberries, quartered

¾ cup Roasted Spicy Pecans

Thyme Vinaigrette:

⅓ cup balsamic vinegar

2 tablespoons Dijon mustard

2 tablespoons honey

2 garlic cloves, minced

2 small shallots, minced

¼ teaspoon crushed lemon thyme

¼ teaspoon salt

¼ teaspoon pepper

¾ cup olive oil

Roasted Spicy Pecans:

¼ cup sugar plus 2 tablespoons sugar, divided

¾ cup hot water

¾ cup pecan halves

1 tablespoon chili powder

⅛ teaspoon ground red pepper

- Rub chicken breasts with olive oil and season well with salt and pepper.
- Grill chicken breasts over medium heat for 20 to 25 minutes, turning once.
- Slice chicken breasts into bite-size strips. Set aside.
- To make Thyme Vinaigrette, whisk together first eight ingredients until well blended.
- Slowly whisk in oil. Toss greens with vinaigrette and half of blue cheese. Set aside.
- To make Spicy Pecans, preheat oven to 350°.
- Dissolve ¼ cup sugar in hot water. Add pecans and soak for 5 minutes. Drain.
- Combine 2 tablespoons sugar, chili powder and red pepper. Add pecans and toss.
- Roast pecans on a lightly greased baking sheet for 10 minutes.
- Place greens on four individual plates. Arrange orange slices, onion slices and strawberries over greens. Top with Roasted Spicy Pecans and remaining blue cheese.
- Hint: Make pecans ahead and store in airtight container until ready to use.

Serves 4

"The best hostess gift—be a great guest!"

Country Ham Salad

An old-fashioned Kentucky favorite!

1 cup cooked country ham, ground

2 tablespoons finely chopped
   celery

1 tablespoon sweet pickle relish,
   well drained

3 tablespoons real mayonnaise

- Mix all ingredients well.
- Serve.
- Note: The sweet pickle relish really enhances the flavor of this salad.

Serves 4

Confetti Chicken Salad with Lime Vinaigrette

Wonderful for a ladies' spring or summer luncheon!

Vinaigrette:

⅓ cup chopped shallots

2 limes, juiced

1 tablespoon minced garlic

½ cup vegetable oil

Salt and pepper

Salad:

3 cups thinly sliced red or green
   leaf lettuce

2 cups thinly sliced purple cabbage

1 cup cooked and shredded
   chicken breast

2 Roma tomatoes, seeded and diced

⅓ cup thinly sliced purple onion

½ red bell pepper, thinly sliced

½ yellow bell pepper, thinly sliced

½ cup crumbled tortilla chips

⅓ cup frozen corn, thawed

½ cup crumbled feta cheese for
   topping

- To make vinaigrette, combine shallots, lime juice and garlic. Gradually whisk in oil and season with salt and pepper.
- Combine all salad ingredients except feta cheese and toss with vinaigrette.
- Top with feta cheese.

Variation: For more flavor, grill chicken and slice thinly.

Serves 6

Chicken Salad Olivier

2 whole bone-in chicken breasts
   (about ¾ pound each)
1 large onion, chopped
2 teaspoons salt, divided
½ cup drained and coarsely
   chopped Polish dill pickles
4 new potatoes, boiled, cooled,
   peeled and thinly sliced
3 hard-boiled eggs, thinly sliced
⅛ teaspoon white pepper
¾ cup mayonnaise
¾ cup sour cream
2 tablespoons capers, drained
1 tablespoon fresh dill (or dried),
   finely cut
Black olives for garnish
Tomato wedges for garnish

- Simmer chicken breasts in a small amount of water with chopped onion and 1 teaspoon of salt until tender. Remove skin and cut meat into ½-inch wide strips.
- Mix chicken, pickles, potatoes and eggs in a large mixing bowl. Sprinkle with remaining salt and white pepper.
- In a small bowl, whip together mayonnaise and sour cream. Mix half into the salad.
- Spread the salad in a 9 x 9-inch pan. Lightly mask the salad with the remaining sour cream/mayonnaise mixture. Wash capers and pat dry. Sprinkle onto salad along with dill.
- Garnish with black olives and tomato wedges. Chill before serving.

Serves 6

Chilly, Nutty Pea Salad

Great for summer picnics!

1 (16 ounce) package frozen
   baby green peas
2 green onions, chopped
½ cup cashews
1 (8 ounce) can sliced water
   chestnuts
1 cup sour cream
½ teaspoon salt
Black pepper to taste

- Mix all ingredients together in a large bowl.
- Cover and refrigerate overnight.

Serves 8

Wild Rice and Chicken Salad

Makes a great dinner with a tossed salad and bread!

3 (4.5 ounce) packages wild rice mix

3 cups cooked bite-size pieces of
    chicken

1 avocado, chopped into bite-size
    pieces

⅓ cup chopped toasted pecans

½ cup chopped red peppers

Dressing:

2 garlic cloves, minced

1 tablespoon Dijon mustard

1 teaspoon salt

¼ teaspoon pepper

¼ teaspoon sugar

⅓ cup seasoned rice vinegar

⅓ cup vegetable oil

1 lemon, juiced

- Prepare wild rice according to package directions. Add chicken, avocado, pecans and peppers.
- Combine dressing ingredients and add to rice. Toss well.
- Chill before serving.

Serves 8 to 10

Salad Parmesan

4 cups fresh broccoli florets

4 cups fresh cauliflower florets

1 large sweet onion, thinly sliced

¼ cup sugar

⅓ cup grated Parmesan cheese

½ teaspoon salt

½ teaspoon basil leaves

2 cups mayonnaise or salad dressing

1 pound bacon, crisply cooked
    and crumbled

1 large head lettuce, torn into
    bite-size pieces

2 cups seasoned croutons

1 (8 ounce) can sliced water
    chestnuts, drained

- In a large bowl, break broccoli and cauliflower into bite-size pieces. Combine with onion.
- In a small bowl, combine sugar, cheese, salt, basil and mayonnaise. Mix well.
- Toss vegetables and dressing.
- Refrigerate for several hours or overnight.
- Just before serving, add bacon, lettuce, croutons and water chestnuts; toss lightly.

Serves 20

Mediterranean Pasta Salad

Good as a main course or side dish!

Dressing:

½ cup olive oil

6 tablespoons fresh lemon juice

¼ cup balsamic vinegar

4 garlic cloves, minced

2 tablespoons fresh minced (or dried) oregano

1 teaspoon mint leaves

1 teaspoon salt

1½ teaspoons freshly ground pepper

Salad:

12 ounces rotini pasta

5 Roma tomatoes, chopped

1 cucumber, peeled, seeded and chopped

5 green onions, chopped

½ cup chopped red onion

1 (14 ounce) can artichoke hearts, chopped or quartered

1 small green pepper, seeded and chopped

1 cup chopped fresh parsley

2 cups crumbled feta cheese

12 pepperoncinis, minced

20-25 kalamata or Greek olives

- Whisk dressing ingredients together. Set aside.
- Cook pasta according to package directions. Drain.
- Combine pasta, tomatoes, cucumbers, green and red onions, artichoke hearts, green pepper, parsley, feta cheese, pepperoncinis and olives in a large bowl.
- Pour dressing over pasta mixture and toss.
- Cover and refrigerate for 3 to 4 hours or overnight to allow flavors to blend.
- Note: Serve with lightly toasted pita bread triangles which have been brushed with olive oil.

Serves 6 to 8

Tri-Color Rotini Salad

Dressing:

¼ cup sugar

¾ cup cider vinegar

¾ cup oil

¼ teaspoon salt

¼ teaspoon pepper

¼ teaspoon accent

¾ teaspoon garlic powder

1 tablespoon parsley flakes

Pasta:

4 cups tri-color rotini

8 ounces cheddar cheese, cubed

1 pint cherry tomatoes

1 (5¾ ounce) can sliced olives, drained

1 (14 ounce) can artichokes (not marinated)

- Combine dressing ingredients in a shaker. Refrigerate; shake occasionally.
- Cook pasta; drain.
- Mix cheese and vegetables; add to pasta.
- Pour dressing over pasta several hours before serving, or pour half on the night before and the remainder on the next morning.
- Note: Dressing will keep for a long time and is also good over salad greens.

Serves 8

Caesar Salad

3 egg yolks

1 (2 ounce) tube anchovy paste or 1 (2 ounce) can anchovies

3 garlic cloves, minced

2 teaspoons Worcestershire sauce

3 tablespoons Dijon mustard

¼ cup red wine vinegar

1 tablespoon freshly cracked black pepper

1 cup extra-virgin olive oil

½ cup freshly grated Parmesan cheese

1 large head romaine lettuce, torn into bite-size pieces

2 cups plain or seasoned croutons

- In a blender, combine egg yolks at low speed.
- Add anchovy paste, garlic, Worcestershire sauce, mustard, vinegar, black pepper, olive oil and Parmesan cheese one at a time, mixing thoroughly.
- Refrigerate dressing for 2 hours.
- Toss lettuce with dressing and sprinkle with croutons.
- Garnish with additional Parmesan cheese and cracked black pepper.
- Note: Add grilled shrimp or chicken for a complete meal.

Serves 6

Poppy Seed Dressing

¾ cup sugar
⅓ cup vinegar
1 cup vegetable oil
1 tablespoon onion juice or
   grated onion
1 teaspoon salt
1 teaspoon dry mustard
1 tablespoon poppy seeds

- Combine all dressing ingredients in a jar; shake well.
- Cover and chill in refrigerator for at least 2 hours.
- Mix or shake well before serving.
- Serve over a green salad.

Yields 2 cups

Dijon Vinaigrette

1 garlic clove, minced
½ teaspoon pepper
½ teaspoon sugar
1 tablespoon Dijon mustard
1 teaspoon Italian seasoning
3 tablespoons wine vinegar
½ cup extra-virgin olive oil

- In a blender, combine garlic, pepper, sugar, mustard, Italian seasoning and vinegar. Blend until smooth.
- Slowly add oil and blend again.
- Serve immediately over a green salad.

Yields ¾ cup

"Lettuce Entertain You" Salad

2 large heads iceberg lettuce, washed, drained and torn into bite-size pieces

1 relish recipe (prepared 24 hours in advance)

1 feta dressing recipe (prepared 24 hours in advance)

3 large fresh tomatoes, peeled and cut into wedges

Relish:

1 (6 ounce) can pitted ripe olives, drained and sliced

1 (16 ounce) can French-style green beans, drained

1 (15 ounce) can young, French peas, drained

1 (12 ounce) can shoe-peg (or tender young) corn, drained

1 medium, Bermuda onion, sliced into thin strips

1 medium red or golden pepper, sliced into thin rings

1 cup thinly sliced celery

½ cup vegetable oil

¼ cup tarragon vinegar

½ cup sugar

2 teaspoons water

½ teaspoon coarsely ground black pepper

Feta Dressing:

1 cup mayonnaise

¼ cup sour cream

2 cups buttermilk

1 (1.4 ounce) package buttermilk farm-style dressing

4 ounces crumbled feta cheese

- Prepare lettuce as instructed; set aside.
- To make relish, combine vegetables in a large mixing bowl suitable for marinating.
- Combine vegetable oil, tarragon vinegar, sugar, water and pepper in a jar. Shake well. Pour over vegetables; cover and let marinate. Refrigerate for 24 hours.
- To prepare feta dressing, whisk mayonnaise, sour cream, buttermilk, and buttermilk dressing together in a large jar. Add feta cheese and stir. Cover and refrigerate for 24 hours.
- Assemble the salad in layers, beginning with a layer of lettuce, then drained relish, tomato and dollops of dressing.
- Note: For a beautiful presentation, use a straight-sided glass bowl.

Serves 12 to 16

"Don't forget to chill the salad plates ahead."

Crunchy Romaine Toss

This is delicious - men love it!

1 cup chopped walnuts

1 package Ramen noodles, uncooked and broken into pieces (discard flavor packet)

4 tablespoons unsalted butter

1 bunch broccoli, coarsely chopped

1 head romaine lettuce, washed and broken into pieces

4 green onions, chopped

Dressing:

1 cup vegetable oil

1 cup sugar

½ cup wine vinegar

3 teaspoons soy sauce

Salt and pepper to taste

- Brown walnuts and noodles in butter; cool on paper towels.
- Mix noodles and walnuts with broccoli, romaine lettuce and onions.
- Blend dressing ingredients together in a small mixing bowl.
- Pour dressing over salad and toss well.
- Note: This can be made ahead; however, do not put noodles and walnuts or dressing onto the salad until ready to serve.
- Note: This salad complements Honey Glazed Pork Chops on page 137.

Serves 6 to 8

Deer Camp Slaw

1 head cabbage, shredded

3 carrots, grated

1 green pepper, sliced into thin rings

1 large sweet onion, sliced into rings

4 tablespoons vegetable oil

¾ cup vinegar

¾ cup water

¾ cup sugar

- Combine cabbage, carrots, peppers and onions in a large mixing bowl.
- Drizzle vegetable oil over vegetables and toss. Set aside.
- Combine vinegar, water and sugar in a saucepan; bring to a boil.
- Pour hot liquid over slaw; press down and cover.
- Refrigerate at least 4 hours before serving.

Serves 6 to 8

Caesar Salad with Tortellini and Asparagus

4 cups water

1 (9 ounce) package refrigerated cheese-filled tortellini, uncooked

½ pound fresh asparagus, trimmed and cut into 2-inch pieces

½ cup lemon juice

6 tablespoons olive oil

4 tablespoons water

2 tablespoons Worcestershire sauce

½ teaspoon freshly ground pepper

2 garlic cloves, minced

1 head romaine lettuce, torn into bite-size pieces

½ cup grated Parmesan cheese

- Bring water to a boil in a large pot. Add tortellini and asparagus; cook for 4 minutes.
- Drain; rinse in cold water and set aside.
- Whisk together lemon juice, olive oil, water, Worcestershire sauce, pepper, and garlic; set aside.
- Place lettuce, tortellini and asparagus in a large serving bowl.
- Add dressing and toss gently.
- Sprinkle with Parmesan.
- Note: Add strips of grilled chicken breast for a light entrée.

Serves 4

Pretty in Pink Salad

A pretty pink salad appropriate for summer gatherings, baby, or bridal showers.

1 (8 ounce) package cream cheese

¾ cup sugar

1 (20 ounce) can sliced pineapple, drained and chopped

1 (8 ounce) can crushed pineapple, drained

1 (10 ounce) package frozen strawberries, thawed and juice reserved

¾ cup chopped pecans

3 bananas, sliced

1 (8 ounce) container non-dairy whipped topping

- Blend cream cheese and sugar.
- Add remaining ingredients and stir well.
- Pour mixture into individual molds or paper-lined muffin tins.
- Freeze until firm; approximately 3 hours.
- Note: Prepare these individual, frozen salads ahead and store in freezer for up to 1 month.

Serves 20

Red Leaf Salad Provençal

Dressing:

1½ tablespoons balsamic
  vinegar

1 teaspoon Dijon mustard

1 teaspoon brown sugar

¼ teaspoon salt

¼ teaspoon pepper

4 tablespoons extra-virgin olive
  oil

Salad:

¼ cup sliced almonds

1 head red leaf lettuce, washed
  and torn into bite-size pieces

10 fresh strawberries, rinsed,
  capped and slivered

Fresh Parmesan cheese, slivered
  for garnish

- To prepare dressing, whisk together balsamic vinegar, mustard, brown sugar, salt and pepper in a small bowl.
- While whisking, slowly add olive oil until dressing is thoroughly combined; set aside.
- Toast almonds in a small skillet over medium heat for 3 minutes. Be careful not to burn. Remove almonds and put into a small bowl. Set aside.
- In a serving bowl, arrange lettuce. Top with strawberry slices and almonds.
- Whisk dressing again and pour over salad; toss gently.
- Garnish with fresh Parmesan cheese slivers.
- Serve immediately.

Variation: For a different taste, substitute ¼ cup crumbled feta cheese for Parmesan. Mixed baby greens may be used instead of red leaf lettuce.

Serves 4 to 6

Avocado and Mushroom Salad

1 head green leaf lettuce

1 avocado

1 (8 ounce) package fresh
  mushrooms

6 tablespoons olive oil

2 tablespoons balsamic vinegar

1 (4 ounce) package crumbled
  blue cheese

- Wash and tear lettuce into pieces. Pat dry; set aside.
- Peel and slice avocado.
- Wash mushrooms and remove stems; slice.
- Mix olive oil and balsamic vinegar in a large bowl. Add lettuce, avocados, mushrooms and blue cheese; toss.

Serves 6

Spinach Mushroom Salad

1½ pounds fresh spinach

½ pound fresh button
    mushrooms

½ cup vegetable oil

3 tablespoons white wine vinegar

1 tablespoon finely chopped
    onion

2 teaspoons Dijon mustard

1 teaspoon salt

1 teaspoon sugar

Dash of pepper

4 bacon slices, cooked and
    crumbled for garnish

- Remove spinach stems. Wash leaves and pat dry. Tear spinach into bite-size pieces; set aside.
- Rinse mushrooms in cold water; drain and pat dry. Thinly slice mushrooms; set aside.
- Combine oil, vinegar, onion, mustard, salt, sugar and pepper in a jar. Shake to blend.
- Combine spinach, mushrooms and dressing in a serving bowl. Toss until spinach is well coated with dressing.
- Garnish salad with bacon.
- Serve immediately.

Serves 6

Red Leaf Balsamic Salad

Dressing:

6 tablespoons olive oil

3 tablespoons balsamic vinegar

1 teaspoon salt

1 teaspoon paprika

2 teaspoons sugar

Salad:

1 head red leaf lettuce

1 purple onion, sliced into thin
    rings

½ cup crumbled gorgonzola
    cheese

- To prepare dressing, whisk all ingredients. Set aside.
- Wash, dry and tear lettuce into bite-size pieces.
- Place lettuce in a serving bowl. Top with onion.
- Drizzle with dressing and toss gently.
- Garnish with gorgonzola cheese.
- Serve immediately.

Serves 4 to 6

Pear and Walnut Salad

An excellent year-round salad.

1 head romaine lettuce, torn
    into pieces
½ cup chopped walnuts
½ fresh pear, peeled, cored and
    thinly sliced
⅓ cup crumbled blue cheese

Dressing:
¼ cup olive oil
¼ cup balsamic vinegar
1 large garlic clove, minced
1 teaspoon sugar
1 teaspoon apple, orange or pear
    juice
1 teaspoon marjoram, ground to
    powder (in palm of hand
    using thumb)

- Mix lettuce, walnuts, pears and blue cheese in a large bowl.
- Mix dressing ingredients; blend well.
- Pour dressing over salad and toss.
- Serve immediately.
- Note: Dressing can be prepared ahead but not do not refrigerate.

Serves 4

Bacon Blue Salad

Dressing:
6 tablespoons olive oil
6 tablespoons vegetable oil
4 tablespoons lemon juice
3 fresh garlic cloves, minced
1 teaspoon Worcestershire sauce
½ cup grated Parmesan cheese

Salad:
1 large head romaine lettuce,
    torn into bite-size pieces
6 bacon slices, cooked and
    crumbled
1 cup crumbled blue cheese

- Combine oil olive, vegetable oil, lemon juice, garlic, Worcestershire sauce and Parmesan cheese in a blender or food processor. Blend until smooth.
- Arrange lettuce in a serving bowl. Toss with desired amount of dressing.
- Garnish with bacon and blue cheese.
- Serve immediately.
- Note: Use the best blue cheese available for a superior flavor. Also, this dressing may be prepared a day in advance and stored in the refrigerator.

Serves 6 to 8

Tomato Aspic

3 cups spicy (or plain) tomato juice

1 celery stalk, chopped

1 teaspoon salt

½ teaspoon pepper

2 lemon slices

1 onion, chopped

2 bay leaves

½ cup vinegar, divided

3 (.25 ounce) envelopes gelatin

⅔ cup cold tomato juice

1 teaspoon Worcestershire sauce

1 tablespoon lemon juice

Mayonnaise seasoned with
   horseradish for topping

- Combine tomato juice, celery, salt, pepper, lemon slices, onions, bay leaves and ¼ cup vinegar; simmer for 12 minutes.
- Strain carefully.
- Stir gelatin into cold tomato juice. Add Worcestershire sauce, ¼ cup vinegar and lemon juice.
- Combine hot mixture with gelatin and pour into a 9-inch square dish.
- Chill until firm.
- Top with mayonnaise seasoned with horseradish.

Variation: Add sliced, stuffed olives to mixture.

Serves 6

Christmas Cranberry-Orange Salad

An old family recipe and holiday tradition.

3 ounces fresh cranberries

1 small orange, unpeeled,
   chopped and seeded

1 cup sugar

1 (11 ounce) can mandarin
   oranges, drained, juice
   reserved

1 (8 ounce) can crushed
   pineapple, drained, juice
   reserved

2 (3 ounce) packages orange
   gelatin

- Wash cranberries and orange. Chop together in a food processor.
- Transfer mixture to a bowl and stir in sugar. Allow to sit for 1 hour.
- Add drained oranges and pineapple to cranberry mixture; set aside.
- Add enough water to reserved orange and pineapple juices to make 1½ cups liquid.
- Bring to a boil in a small saucepan. Remove from heat.
- Mix liquid with 2 packages gelatin to dissolve gelatin. Allow to cool.
- Add gelatin to fruit mixture and stir well.
- Pour mixture into a square 9-inch pan or individual molds. Chill until ready to serve.

Variation: Double ingredients and chill in a 9 x 13-inch casserole to serve 24.

Serves 12

Spiced Cranberry-Raisin Chutney

Very colorful for a holiday table and wonderful with grilled pork.

2 cups water

3 cups sugar

2 oranges, unpeeled, chopped
 and seeded

1 teaspoon fresh ginger or
 crystallized ginger, crushed

4 cups fresh cranberries

1 teaspoon cinnamon

½ teaspoon ground cloves

1 cinnamon stick

1 cup raisins

- Combine water and sugar in a large saucepan; bring to a boil, stirring occasionally.
- Place oranges in a blender and process until finely chopped.
- Add oranges and ginger to saucepan; reduce heat and simmer uncovered for 20 minutes.
- Add cranberries, cinnamon, cloves and cinnamon stick to saucepan. Simmer uncovered until thick.
- Add raisins and cook until mixture bubbles, about 5 to 8 minutes.
- Remove from heat and transfer mixture to a bowl; cool. Remove cinnamon stick.
- Cover and refrigerate several hours to allow flavors to increase.
- Chutney will keep in the refrigerator for 1 week.
- Serve at room temperature.

Serves 10 to 15

"I may be old-fashioned, but I still believe in party favors. One of the most appreciated and inexpensive choices was small, raffia-tied bags of homemade potpourri! I included dried flowers, seedpods, and herbs. The best part was that it all came out of my own backyard."

ENTRÉES

Party Thyme

Party Thyme

Paducah has always known when it is time to celebrate—anytime! Through the years, however, lifestyles have changed, and so have thyme worn traditions of entertaining. Today's women, involved in careers and family activities, have no time to don white gloves and polish silver for formal teas or bridge parties. "Dressy casual," describing all aspects of party giving from food and table decor to appropriate attire, has become the preferred mode of entertaining. Spouses, and sometimes children, have become involved when it's party thyme. Rites of passage such as births and weddings are still enthusiastically embraced. However, the ubiquitous female-only bridal and baby showers have evolved into lively parties involving couples, with the happy future husband or father-to-be as important a fixture as the female guest of honor.

Wedding receptions are no longer the stiff and formal punch and wedding cake affairs. Guests can expect a buffet of entrees, sides and salads, and dancing to live music until the wee hours. After all, these are events to be celebrated with gusto and great food. Great does not necessarily mean gourmet, however. The food can be as simple as fried chicken, country ham, and barbecue, accompanied by grits, "cooked down" green beans, and even turnip greens. Other thymeless traditions are pre-nuptial parties, and in summer, family reunions and garden parties.

Although certain traditions may have changed, one thing still remains—hospitality is synonymous with entertaining in Paducah. Party givers generously open their homes to treat guests to lavish buffet suppers, festive cocktail parties, and elegant sit-down dinners. Whether casual or formal, gracious hosts and hostesses pay careful attention to detail to insure their guests have a grand thyme.

Cocktail Party

Extraordinary Crab Dip
Crispy Pesto Shrimp
Miniature Sausage Quiches
Sun-Dried Tomato Basil Terrine
Madeira Mushrooms
Prosciutto-Wrapped Asparagus
Beef Tenderloin on the Grill
Top Hat Strawberries
Miniature Cherry Bon-Bon Cheesecakes

Elegant Dinner Party

Almond Pinecones
Avocado Salmon Rolls
Bacon Blue Salad
Elegant Beef Tenderloin
with Creamy Horseradish Sauce
Lemon Vinaigrette Asparagus
Potatoes Lyonnaise
Sour Cream Dinner Rolls
Chocolate Mousse Terrine
with Raspberry Coulis

Party Thyme Ideas:

Cheers: Hosts should always be prepared to toast the guests of honor. Although, spontaneous salutes are welcome, too.

Salute: When selecting beverages, have appropriate glasses for the most popular drinks. Martinis lose some of their mystique when served in a plastic cup.

Elegant Beef Tenderloin
with Creamy Horseradish Sauce

Simple but elegant. *A good Merlot complements this dish.*

2 tablespoons Creole seasoning

1 (4 to 4½ pound) beef
    tenderloin

1 tablespoon olive oil

3 tablespoons Worcestershire
    sauce

3 tablespoons chopped fresh
    garlic

2 tablespoons horseradish

½ teaspoon lemon juice

3 tablespoons Dijon mustard or
    Creole mustard

2 teaspoons cracked black
    pepper

Horseradish Sauce:

½ cup mayonnaise

½ cup whipping cream

Tabasco sauce to taste

Worcestershire sauce to taste

⅛ teaspoon dry mustard

⅓ cup horseradishes, well
    drained

- Preheat oven to 400°.
- Rub Creole seasoning on tenderloin. Heat olive oil in a large skillet. Sear tenderloin in hot skillet for two minutes on each side.
- Place tenderloin in a large roasting pan.
- Mix Worcestershire sauce, garlic, horseradish, lemon juice, mustard and pepper. Rub well over tenderloin. If any sauce remains, pour over meat.
- Insert meat thermometer into tenderloin. Bake for 30 to 35 minutes. Remove when thermometer reads 130° to 140° for medium-rare meat.
- Remove from pan and place on a serving dish immediately to avoid further cooking.
- To make horseradish sauce, mix all ingredients together; carefully adjust to taste.
- Chill for several hours before serving.
- Slice beef and serve with sauce.

Variation: Serve sliced tenderloin on rolls for a cocktail buffet.

Serves 8

> "If you build, put in a double oven. If you remodel your kitchen, put in a double oven."

Roasted Prime Rib

1 4-rib standing rib roast
(trimmed 10 to 10½ pounds)

¼ cup unsalted butter, softened
and cut into pieces

¼ cup plus 1 tablespoon flour

2 teaspoons coarsely ground
white pepper

1 teaspoon salt

1 tablespoon finely ground black
peppercorns

1½ bay leaves, crumbled

- Let roast stand at room temperature for 1 hour.
- Preheat oven to 500°.
- Combine butter, flour, white pepper, salt, ground peppercorns and bay leaves to form a paste.
- Rub the meat with the paste. Place meat in a large roasting pan, rib side down. Bake for 30 minutes.
- Reduce heat to 350° and roast for 1 hour and 45 minutes-2 hours longer or until a meat thermometer registers 130° for medium-rare meat.
- Let roast sit for at least 20 minutes before carving.
- Note: Try serving with Roasted Rosemary New Potatoes on page 158 and Lemon Vinaigrette Asparagus on page 148.

Italian Roast Beef Sandwiches

Great for a tailgate party.

1 (3 pound) lean beef roast

1 package zesty Italian dressing
mix

1 package dry onion soup mix

2 (10¾ ounce) cans beef broth

1 (10 ounce) jar pepperoncini
peppers

Mozzarella cheese, sliced

6 hoagie-style rolls

- Combine roast, Italian dressing mix, onion soup mix, beef broth, and half of peppers in a slow cooker; cook for about 8 hours (meat will fall apart easily).
- Serve with mozzarella cheese and pepperoncini peppers on hoagie-style rolls.

Serves 4 to 6

Peppered Red Wine Filet Mignon

Just right for an intimate dinner.

4 (6 to 8 ounce) beef tenderloin
    fillets
1 teaspoon salt
2 teaspoons black pepper
¼ cup crushed green
    peppercorns, drained
2 tablespoons Dijon mustard
4 tablespoons butter

Sauce:
¾ cup red wine
1 cup heavy cream
Parsley for garnish

- Sprinkle fillets with salt and pepper. Mix crushed peppercorns with Dijon mustard and spread on both sides of steaks, pressing peppercorns into meat.

- In a large skillet, melt butter on high heat. Add fillets and sear one minute per side. Remove fillets.

- Reduce heat to medium and return fillets to the pan. Continue cooking for 3 to 5 minutes per side for medium rare or 8 to 10 minutes for well-done meat.

- Remove steaks from skillet. Keep warm.

- Add red wine slowly to skillet while scraping down the sides of pan. Reduce heat to low and slowly add cream. Simmer 2 minutes, stirring constantly.

- Serve over steaks.

Serves 4

Chicken Monterey

4 boneless chicken breast halves
Salt and pepper to taste
4 tablespoons olive oil
1 lime, juiced
1 large onion, sliced
1 green pepper, sliced
1 red pepper, sliced
1 (8 ounce) brick Monterey Jack
    cheese, sliced

- Preheat oven to 350°.

- Pound chicken breasts slightly and sprinkle with salt and pepper.

- Sauté chicken in olive oil over medium heat until golden brown on both sides.

- Place chicken in a 9 x 13-inch baking dish. Sprinkle with lime juice and bake for 30 minutes.

- Sauté onion and peppers in olive oil until tender.

- Remove chicken from oven and top each breast with several slices of onions, peppers and 2 or 3 slices of cheese.

- Bake for an additional 5 to 10 minutes.

Serves 4

Chicken Breasts in Phyllo for Eight

4 whole large chicken breasts

½ pound phyllo

¾ cup butter, divided

**Green Peppercorn
and Spinach Stuffing:**

2 cups chopped spinach leaves

1 cup shredded Swiss cheese

½ cup ricotta cheese

½ medium onion, chopped

2 hard-boiled eggs, chopped

1 garlic clove, crushed

2 heaping teaspoons crushed
    green peppercorns

½ teaspoon salt

Pink Madeira Sauce:

2 tablespoons butter or
    margarine

2 tablespoons flour

2 tablespoons Madeira

1 cup chicken broth

2 teaspoons tomato paste

⅓ cup sour cream

⅓ cup chopped chives or green
    onion tops

½ teaspoon salt

White pepper to taste

- Pound chicken breasts until very thin. Sprinkle with salt and pepper.
- To make Green Peppercorn and Spinach Stuffing, mix all ingredients together until well blended in a very large bowl.
- Spread ⅓ cup of stuffing over each chicken breast. Beginning at one end, roll up once; fold in sides and roll as for a jelly roll. Place 1 sheet of phyllo on a damp towel. (Keep remaining phyllo covered while not using.) Melt ½ cup butter; brush phyllo with butter; fold in half widthwise. Turn phyllo so narrow end faces you. Place one rolled chicken breast two inches from end of phyllo.
- Top chicken with ½ tablespoon cold butter. Roll phyllo over chicken once and fold in sides. Continue rolling to end of phyllo.
- Place on a rimmed baking sheet seam side down. Brush top with butter. Repeat with remaining chicken and phyllo.
- Preheat oven to 400°.
- To make Pink Madeira Sauce, melt butter in a medium saucepan. Add flour and cook, stirring until mixture is golden. Remove from heat and whisk in Madeira and chicken broth.
- Return to heat and cook, stirring until mixture boils and thickens.
- In a small bowl, mix tomato paste and sour cream. Add a little of the hot sauce to the bowl, mixing thoroughly; return to saucepan.
- Stir in chopped chives, salt and pepper.
- Bake chicken breasts for 25 to 30 minutes or until golden.
- Drizzle with Pink Madeira Sauce.

Serves 8

Smoked Gouda and Pesto Filled Chicken

4 boneless chicken breast halves
½ cup grated smoked Gouda
⅓ cup ready-made pesto sauce
2 tablespoons toasted pine nuts
1 teaspoon minced green onions
⅓ cup flour
2 tablespoons olive oil

- Preheat oven to 350°.
- Pound chicken breasts between sheets of waxed paper. Mix Gouda, pesto, pine nuts and green onions in a small bowl.
- Spread 2 tablespoons of cheese mixture on top of each chicken breast, roll tightly, and secure with toothpick.
- Dredge chicken in flour. Sauté rolled chicken in heated oil on medium-high heat for 6 minutes and until golden brown, turning occasionally.
- Place chicken in a pan and bake for 20 minutes and until chicken is tender and cooked throughout.

Serves 4

Sour Cream Chicken

2 garlic cloves, minced
1 cup sour cream
2 tablespoons lemon juice
½ teaspoon salt
½ teaspoon paprika
1 teaspoon hot sauce
4 boneless chicken breasts
1 cup seasoned bread crumbs
½ cup butter, melted

- Combine garlic, sour cream, lemon juice, salt, paprika and hot sauce.
- Pour over chicken and marinate overnight.
- Preheat oven to 350°.
- Coat chicken breasts with bread crumbs. Place in a greased baking dish.
- Pour melted butter over chicken and bake for 1 hour.

Serves 4

"For my husband's retirement party, we set up several dining and drinking stations throughout the house to accommodate the large number of guests. Our beverages were placed in a long hallway that allowed an easy entrance and exit for our guests. And since most guests tend to flock to one particular area, we placed the dessert bar in the largest room of the house—the GARAGE! It was a hit!"

Southern Chicken and Cheese Grits

Roux:

½ cup flour

½ cup vegetable oil

2 garlic cloves, minced

1 onion, chopped

1 green pepper, chopped

1 (8 ounce) can tomato sauce

3 bay leaves

1 (10¾ ounce) can chicken broth

Cheese Grits:

7 cups water

2 cups quick-cooking grits

1 teaspoon salt

Dash garlic salt (optional)

12 ounces processed cheese,
   cubed or shredded

Chicken:

3 tablespoons flour

1 teaspoon ground red pepper

½ teaspoon garlic salt

½ teaspoon thyme

1 teaspoon oregano

1 teaspoon pepper

2 pounds chicken breasts, diced
   into bite-size pieces

3 tablespoons vegetable oil

- To make roux, combine flour and oil in a large pot. Cook mixture, stirring constantly, on medium-low heat for 20 to 30 minutes or until the roux is the color of caramel.
- Add garlic, onion and green pepper. Sauté for 4 to 5 minutes, then add tomato sauce, bay leaves and chicken broth.
- Cover and simmer on low heat for 20 minutes. While the roux is simmering, prepare cheese grits.
- Bring water to a boil. Stir in grits and salt. Boil again then reduce heat and simmer for 4 minutes, stirring constantly.
- Add cheese and stir until melted.
- To prepare chicken, combine flour, red pepper, garlic salt, thyme, oregano and pepper, blending well.
- Dredge chicken in flour mixture. Heat vegetable oil in a nonstick skillet on medium. In small batches, brown the chicken on all sides.
- Place the chicken in the roux. Cover and simmer on low for 5 minutes. Remove the bay leaves and serve over cheese grits.

Variation: This entrée can be served different ways:

- *Press cheese grits into a greased ring mold. Let stand for 10 to 15 minutes. Invert onto a serving platter. Pour chicken into the center of the molded grits and serve.*
- *Press cheese grits into 1 greased 9-inch cake pan. Let stand for 10 to 15 minutes. Cut into wedges and place on a plate with the chicken poured over the grits.*

Serves 6 to 9

Chicken à la King

A wonderful dish for luncheons or showers.

2 cups sliced fresh mushrooms
2 small green peppers, finely chopped
2 tablespoons butter
6 cups chicken, cooked and diced
2 (2 ounce) cans pimentos, finely
   chopped
2 cups finely chopped celery
1 cup blanched almonds

Cream Sauce:
1 cup butter
1 cup less 1 tablespoon flour
4 cups chicken stock, strained
1 cup half-and-half
1 egg yolk, slightly beaten
5 tablespoons dry sherry
Toast points for topping

- Sauté mushrooms and green peppers in butter for 5 minutes. Remove from heat.
- Mix in chicken, pimentos, celery and almonds.
- For cream sauce, melt butter over medium heat. Slowly add flour, stirring until smooth. Add stock, half-and-half and egg yolk. Stir until thickened.
- Mix cream sauce with chicken and other ingredients; add sherry.
- Serve in chafing dish with toast points.

Variation: May add one cup of green peas.

Serves 20

Almond Chicken Sauté

¼ cup flour
Salt and pepper to taste
4 bone-in chicken breasts
1 (2 ounce) package sliced almonds
¼ cup margarine
2 teaspoons chicken bouillon
   granules
1 cup hot water
1 teaspoon coarsely ground
   pepper blend
¼ cup white wine

- Mix salt, pepper and flour. Dredge chicken in flour; set aside.
- Sauté almonds in margarine on medium heat until golden brown. Remove almonds. Set aside.
- Brown chicken in remaining margarine. While browning, dissolve bouillon in hot water.
- Sprinkle pepper blend on chicken; reduce heat to simmer. Cover and simmer for 10 minutes. Add white wine and bouillon; simmer another 5 to 10 minutes.
- Place chicken on a platter for serving and top with almonds.

Serves 4

Orange Curry Chicken

4 boneless chicken breasts

¾ cup flour

3 tablespoons fresh ground black pepper

1 tablespoon olive oil

1 tablespoon butter

2 vegetable bouillon cubes

1½ cups water

½ cup orange juice

1 tablespoon curry powder

1 tablespoon cornstarch

- Pound chicken flat between pieces of wax paper.
- Dredge chicken in flour and pepper.
- Brown chicken in oil and butter in a skillet over medium-high heat for 6 to 7 minutes.
- Place chicken on an oven-proof platter in a 200° oven.
- Using the same skillet, heat bouillon cubes, water, orange juice, curry powder and corn starch over medium heat for 8 minutes or until slightly thickened.
- Return chicken to skillet and coat with sauce.
- Serve immediately with rice.

Serves 4

Roasted Cornish Hens with Thyme

4 Cornish game hens, 1 to 1½ pounds

Fresh ground black pepper to taste

2 tablespoons unsalted butter, melted

8 teaspoons fresh chopped lemon thyme, divided

1 teaspoon grated lemon zest

1 teaspoon dried oregano, crumbled

4 garlic cloves, minced and divided

1 lemon, sliced

½ cup melted butter for basting

- Preheat oven to 425°.
- Rinse hens and thoroughly pat dry. Sprinkle cavity with pepper.
- Loosen skin over breasts, being careful not to tear skin.
- Mix melted butter, 4 teaspoons lemon thyme, lemon zest, oregano and half of the garlic until it forms a paste.
- Place paste carefully under the skin of each hen. Place remaining garlic and thyme into each cavity along with lemon slices.
- Truss the hens and place on a rack in a roasting pan. Baste with melted butter. Bake for 45 to 60 minutes or until temperature on a meat thermometer reaches 180° in the thickest part of the thigh.
- Remove truss and serve immediately.

Serves 4

Chicken Piccata

1½ pounds boneless chicken
   tenders
½ cup flour
½ teaspoon salt
½ teaspoon white pepper
2 tablespoons olive oil
1 chicken bouillon cube
¼ cup water
2 tablespoons capers
¾ cup white wine

- Pound chicken tenders until thin. Dredge in flour, salt and pepper.
- Brown a few pieces of chicken at a time in oil.
- Dissolve bouillon cube in water. Mix in with capers and white wine.
- Scrape drippings loose in skillet. Return chicken to skillet and pour sauce over top.
- Cover and simmer 15 minutes.
- Serve with lightly buttered angel hair pasta on the side.

Serves 4

The South's Best Fried Turkey

Great for large gatherings of family or friends.

5 gallons peanut oil
1 (14 to 15 pound) turkey
½ pint injector seasoning
Salt and pepper to taste
1 tablespoon cayenne pepper
1 large onion, thickly sliced
2 celery stalks, sliced 3-inches in
   length
4 fresh garlic cloves, whole
Equipment needed:
1 large, deep 10-gallon turkey
   frying pot with an outside
   propane burner
1 thermometer

- Preheat oil over propane burner (outdoors) to 325°.
- With needle injector, inject turkey with ½ pint of injector seasoning. Make sure to inject all over turkey. Season cavity with salt, pepper and cayenne.
- Slice onion and celery; place in cavity. Place whole garlic cloves into cavity. Thoroughly rub outside of turkey with salt and pepper.
- Lower turkey into frying pot and cook for 25 minutes. Keep the thermometer in the pot so the temperature does not rise.
- Turn bird after 25 minutes and continue cooking for 15 additional minutes. Watch carefully that turkey does not burn.
- Carefully remove bird and check for doneness (it may need an additional 5 minutes). When done, the turkey will be very dark (nearly black) on the outside but moist on the inside.
- Slice and serve.
- Note: Allow oil to cool for several hours before disposing. Oil may be reused to fry fish or chicken.

Serves 10

Turkey Scallopini with Leeks, Currants and Marsala

This is a low-fat dish.

3 large leeks (white and pale
    green parts only), halved and
    sliced lengthwise (about 6
    cups)

2 cups chicken stock or canned
    low-salt broth, divided

2 teaspoons sugar

1 bay leaf

½ teaspoon dried thyme

¼ teaspoon dried rubbed sage

Salt to taste

Pepper to taste

⅓ cup plus 1 teaspoon sweet
    Marsala wine, divided

¼ cup currants

2 tablespoons long grain white
    rice

1 pound turkey cutlets

½ teaspoon minced orange peel

Fresh sage leaves and orange
    peel strips

- Combine leeks, ⅓ cup chicken stock, sugar, bay leaf, thyme and sage in a heavy skillet; season with salt and pepper. Cover and cook over low heat for 25 minutes or until leaks are very tender, stirring occasionally.

- Uncover and cook for 8 minutes or until golden brown and liquid evaporates, stirring frequently. Discard bay leaf. Cover and refrigerate. (This can be prepared a day ahead; reheat before using.)

- Combine ⅓ cup Marsala and ¼ cup currants in a bowl. Let stand for 30 minutes.

- Place remaining chicken stock in a small saucepan. Strain Marsala from currants into stock; reserve currants.

- Bring stock mixture to a boil. Add white rice and reduce heat; cover and simmer for 30 minutes or until rice is very tender.

- Drain rice, reserving stock mixture. Transfer rice and ¼ cup stock mixture to a blender and purée. Add remaining stock mixture and purée until sauce is smooth.

- Heat a large, nonstick skillet over medium-high heat. Season turkey with salt and pepper. Add turkey to skillet and sauté until cooked through and golden brown (about 2 minutes per side).

- Transfer turkey to a plate and tent with foil to keep warm. Add sauce, currants, remaining Marsala and orange peel to the skillet; bring to a boil. Cook for 2 minutes or until sauce thickens.

- Spoon leek mixture onto plates; top with turkey and sauce. Garnish with fresh sage leaves and orange strips.

Serves 4

Rosemary Lamb Chops

1 cup Dijon mustard
8 small bone-in lamb chops
2 cups plain breadcrumbs
3 tablespoons fresh rosemary
2 garlic cloves, minced
2 eggs, beaten
Salt and pepper to taste

- Preheat oven to 450°.
- Thoroughly rub mustard on both sides of lamb chops.
- Combine bread crumbs, rosemary and garlic; mix well.
- Dip chops in egg then roll in breadcrumbs. Place in a baking dish and sprinkle with salt and pepper.
- Bake for 20 to 25 minutes.

Serves 4

Tangy Orange Pork Chops

4 butterfly pork chops
1-2 tablespoons oil
1 (11 ounce) can Mandarin oranges (reserve juice)
5 tablespoons brown sugar
¼ teaspoon cinnamon
¼ teaspoon nutmeg
½ teaspoon salt
1 teaspoon prepared mustard
¼ cup ketchup
1 tablespoon vinegar

- Brown pork chops in oil in a large skillet.
- Add drained oranges to skillet, reserve juice.
- Combine ¾ cup of reserved juice with brown sugar, cinnamon, nutmeg, salt, mustard, ketchup and vinegar. Pour over pork chops.
- Simmer gently until pork is done, approximately 30 minutes.

Serves 4

> *"At one of the best dinner parties I ever attended, I was not seated by my husband, with whom I am predictably comfortable, but by someone I had just met. We had the most engaging conversation. In fact, the hostess' dining room was buzzing with conversation because she had invited an eclectic group of guests and wasn't afraid to be creative with her seating plan."*

Pork Scallops in Dijon Wine Sauce

1¼ pounds boneless pork cutlets
1 tablespoon butter
1 tablespoon vegetable oil
¼ cup dry white wine
½ cup chicken broth
1 cup heavy whipping cream
1 teaspoon Dijon mustard
Salt and pepper

- Pound pork cutlets between two pieces of wax paper to ¼-inch thickness.
- Heat butter and oil in a large skillet over medium-high heat. Add pork cutlets. Cook 4 to 5 minutes on each side until brown. Remove and keep warm.
- Empty fat from skillet. Add wine and chicken broth; cook over high heat for one minute, scraping bits from the bottom.
- Add cream and boil, uncovered, until reduce to about ¾ cup. Remove from heat and whisk in mustard. Pour sauce over pork.

Serves 4 to 6

Extra Tender Barbecued Ribs

3-4 pounds pork spare ribs or
  baby back ribs
1 cup maple syrup
⅓ cup soy sauce
3 tablespoons sherry or cooking
  wine
1 tablespoon garlic powder
2 teaspoons salt
½ teaspoon sugar

- In a large Dutch oven, cover ribs with water and bring to a boil; reduce heat and simmer 45 minutes.
- Preheat oven to 325°.
- Drain ribs; place in a lightly greased 9 x 13-inch pan.
- Mix remaining ingredients and pour over ribs. Bake uncovered for 60-70 minutes, turning once and basting with sauce.
- Let stand 10 minutes before serving.

Serves 3

Company Veal Scallopini

Excellent with Pine Nut Rice (page 159) and Roasted Asparagus Parmesan (page 149).

1½ pounds baby milk-fed veal
¼ cup flour
½ cup Parmesan cheese
1 teaspoon salt
⅛ teaspoon pepper
4 tablespoons butter, divided
3 tablespoons olive oil, divided
½ cup minced onion
¼ cup dry white wine
⅔ cup beef bouillon
¾ pound fresh mushrooms,
    sliced
Parsley for garnish

- Cut veal into 6 thin slices across the grain. Flatten each slice between sheets of wax paper by pounding gently with a mallet until slices are ¼-inch thick.

- Pat slices with paper towels until thoroughly dry.

- Combine flour, Parmesan cheese, salt and pepper. Sprinkle each veal slice with flour mixture and gently press into meat.

- Heat 2 tablespoons butter and 1 tablespoon olive oil in a large, nonstick skillet. Sauté veal slices for 4 to 5 minutes on each side until lightly browned. Remove veal to a warm platter.

- In the same skillet, add 1 tablespoon butter and 1 tablespoon olive oil and sauté onions, cooking slowly for 1 minute.

- Pour wine and beef bouillon into skillet. Boil rapidly to reduce liquid to about ¼ cup, stirring with a wooden spoon.

- Return veal slices to skillet and simmer for 5 to 10 minutes. Meanwhile, sauté mushrooms in 1 tablespoon butter and 1 tablespoon olive oil. Add to veal.

- Garnish with parsley.

This is also delicious when made with chicken.

Serves 4 to 6

"The ornaments of the house are the guests who frequent it."

Anonymous

Louisiana Shrimp

Great served with fresh French bread!

¾ pound large shrimp, peeled
    and deveined

3 tablespoons butter

1 teaspoon chili powder

1 teaspoon freshly ground black
    pepper

⅛ teaspoon cayenne pepper

1 teaspoon minced garlic

2 teaspoons Worcestershire
    sauce

2 tablespoons dry red wine

¼ teaspoon salt

2 bay leaves

- Preheat oven to 400°.
- Place shrimp in one layer in a 9 x 13-inch baking dish.
- Combine remaining ingredients in a saucepan; boil.
- Pour mixture over shrimp and bake for 8 to 10 minutes or until just firm.

Serves 2

Italian Shrimp

Outstanding and easy!

6 tablespoons butter

6 ounces olive oil

½ cup Italian dressing

6 garlic cloves, minced

1 teaspoon hot pepper

¼ cup Worcestershire sauce

7 bay leaves

1 teaspoon salt

1 teaspoon paprika

1 teaspoon pepper

Dash of oregano

Dash of rosemary

2 pounds shrimp, peeled and
    deveined

3 ounces white wine

- Melt butter in a large skillet.
- Mix in oil.
- Add remaining ingredients except shrimp and white wine.
- Cook over medium heat until sauce boils. Reduce heat to low.
- Add shrimp and simmer for 15 minutes.
- Add wine and simmer an additional 10 minutes.
- Serve over hot rice or couscous.

Serves 6

Spinach-Shrimp Parmesan

1 (10 ounce) package frozen
   chopped spinach, cooked and
   drained
1 pound shrimp (with shells)
3 tablespoons butter
3 tablespoons flour
1 cup light cream
½ cup Parmesan cheese
¼ cup sherry
Salt and pepper to taste

- Cook spinach as directed; salt and pepper to taste.
- Place spinach in the bottom of a 1-quart baking dish or five baking shells.
- Boil shrimp (with shells) in salted water for 15 minutes. Let stand in water for 15 minutes; drain and peel.
- Place shrimp on top of spinach. If using baking shells, top with 5 or 6 shrimp.
- Melt butter in a saucepan; slowly add flour, then cream. Stir until thick.
- Add Parmesan and sherry.
- Pour sauce over the shrimp and broil for 5 minutes until brown and bubbly. Watch carefully! If using shells, place on a cookie sheet.

Serves 4

Parmesan Crusted Orange Roughy

An easy dish that looks good enough for company.

2 pounds orange roughy fillets

2 tablespoons fresh lemon juice

½ cup freshly grated Parmesan cheese

4 tablespoons butter

3 tablespoons mayonnaise

3 tablespoons chopped green onion

¼ teaspoon salt

Dash Tabasco sauce

Dash pepper

- Preheat broiler.
- Butter a 9 x 13-inch metal baking dish.
- Place fillets in a single layer in baking dish.
- Brush with lemon juice; let stand for 10 minutes.
- Broil fish 3 to 4 inches under broiler until done.
- Mix remaining ingredients in a bowl; spread over fish.
- Broil for 2 to 3 additional minutes; watch closely.

Serves 4

"After our son was born, I remember thinking, 'we'll never entertain again.' A party for adults and children brings on a whole new set of challenges. We've survived many gatherings and learned early on that the food, drinks, and the activities must be appropriate for children of all ages."

Mini-Crab Cakes with Spicy Mustard Sauce

Makes an incredible appetizer, too!

1 pound lump crabmeat
1¾ cups bread crumbs, divided
1 hard-cooked egg, minced
2 large eggs, lightly beaten
¼ cup minced onion
¼ cup minced red bell pepper
¼ cup minced green bell pepper
1 teaspoon salt
1 teaspoon dry mustard
¼ teaspoon cayenne pepper
Ground black pepper to taste
5 tablespoons butter

Sauce:
1 cup Dijon mustard
¼ cup mayonnaise
Cayenne pepper to taste

- Mix crabmeat, ¾ cup bread crumbs, eggs, onion, peppers, and seasonings.
- Cover and refrigerate for 1½ hours or until firm.
- When mixture is firm, form into 24 balls.
- Coat each ball with remaining bread crumbs.
- Melt butter over medium heat in a large skillet. Sauté crab cakes in batches for 4 to 5 minutes on each side or until brown on all sides.
- Mix ingredients to make sauce; refrigerate. Serve with crab cakes.

Yields 24 mini-crab cakes

"I've celebrated many occasions over the years and long ago, I began a scrapbook of sorts for each of my celebrations. I have saved every invitation and placed the guest lists and menu selections in a small log book. And I even make little follow-up notes after each party. It's a little time consuming at first, but it is such a time saver now. My party book holds great memories of good times past and great ideas for celebrations to come."

Crabmeat Au Gratin

1 cup finely chopped onion

¼ cup finely chopped green pepper

1 celery stalk, finely chopped

¼ cup butter

1 teaspoon salt

½ teaspoon cayenne pepper

½ teaspoon black pepper

½ cup flour

1 cup grated cheddar cheese

½ cup grated mozzarella cheese

1 (12 ounce) can evaporated milk

2 egg yolks

½ cup chopped parsley

½ cup chopped green onions

1 pound fresh lump crabmeat

- Preheat oven to 350°.
- Sauté onions, green pepper and celery in butter. Cover and simmer for 10 minutes being careful not to burn.
- Add salt, cayenne and black pepper.
- Blend in flour and cheeses.
- Cook over medium heat until cheese melts.
- Add evaporated milk, stirring constantly.
- Mix egg yolks slowly into mixture and cook over low heat until creamy. Remove from heat.
- Add parsley, green onions and crabmeat.
- Spray casserole dish with nonstick cooking spray; pour mixture into baking dish.
- Bake for 20 minutes.
- Serve immediately.
- Note: This dish can be prepared ahead prior to baking.

Serves 4 to 6

Poached Salmon with Fresh Dill

Sauce:
½ *cup mayonnaise*
½ *tablespoon lemon juice*
2 *tablespoons minced chives*
½ *cup Dijon mustard*
¾ *cup minced fresh dill, divided*
1 *lemon sliced for garnish*

Salmon:
½ *cup dry white wine*
1½ *cups water*
1 *lemon, sliced*
6 *fresh dill sprigs*
10 *peppercorns*
4 *(6 to 8 ounce) salmon fillets*

- Mix mayonnaise, lemon juice, chives, mustard and ½ cup minced dill to make dill sauce; refrigerate for 1 hour.
- Pour wine and water into a large frying pan.
- Add lemon slices, dill sprigs and peppercorns.
- Bring liquid to a gentle boil and add salmon fillets.
- Reduce heat and simmer for 3 to 4 minutes.
- Turn fillets over and simmer for 3 to 4 additional minutes or until they begin to flake; do not overcook.
- Remove from liquid and place on plates.
- Spoon dill sauce over fillets or use on the side.
- Sprinkle with remaining chopped dill and garnish with lemon slices.
- Note: Dill sauce will keep in the refrigerator for at least 2 days.

Serves 4

"My husband and I usually entertain with three other couples. And our long standing tradition among the couples is treating ourselves to caviar and smoked salmon pâté. We take turns providing it at each party, and what a treat it is! Old friendships are worth a little pampering."

PASTA AND CASSEROLES

Three Quarter Thyme

Three Quarter Thyme

Local music lovers enthusiastically support the Paducah Symphony, not only in concert attendance, but also in financial backing. The Symphony League has raised funds through Symphony Balls, Father-Daughter Balls, and Overture Dinners held in the homes of League members. The most popular fundraiser is a Summer Pops concert held in historic downtown Paducah. The setting lends to the event's informality. Artist Robert Dafford's historical floodwall murals serve as the backdrop for the orchestra. To make the evening fun and festive, the table decorations are based on a theme—a garden party, a tropical luau, or a Broadway show, for instance—and prizes are awarded for originality and creativity. Food is very much a part of the festive evening, and elaborate entrées are planned. A luau group may dress in tropical shirts and grass skirts and serve Polynesian food. Another group might choose a Mexican entrée, don sombreros, and drape colorful serapes on table covers. While these are casual settings, some formally attired couples may be seated at tables decorated with silver candelabras and beautiful floral centerpieces.

An evening at the Paducah Symphony Summer Pops Concert is thyme to be creative—in costume, in table decor, and in food.

Sunset Symphony Picnic

Layered Cheese Torte

Avocado and Mushroom Salad

Sesame Garlic Grilled Pork Tenderloin

Marinated Summer Vegetables

Not for Tea-Thyme Scones

Kahlúa Cake

Notes for a Three Quarter Thyme Party:

High or Low: Be aware of food temperatures when entertaining outdoors. Protect meat, fish, cheese, pasta salads, and fruit salads from discoloration and spoilage by shielding them from the sun.

Music to the ears: Make sure music selections are appropriate in style and volume. End your sunset picnic on a high note and bring along several trash bags, paper towels, and anti-bacterial wipes for the clean-up.

Spicy Southwest Penne

This also makes a great cold salad!

10 Roma tomatoes, blanched, peeled, seeded and diced

Salt to taste

2 tablespoons minced garlic

⅓ cup olive oil

⅓ cup chopped red onion

Juice of 2 limes

1 jalapeño pepper, seeded and minced

4 tablespoons tomato paste

2 teaspoons chili powder

12 ounces penne pasta

1 cup crumbled feta cheese, divided

Pepper to taste

- Place diced tomatoes in a large bowl and salt well.
- In a large skillet, sauté garlic in oil over medium-high heat.
- Pour over tomatoes and toss.
- Blend in onion, lime juice, jalapeño, tomato paste and chili powder. (This can be prepared one hour ahead.)
- Let stand at room temperature.
- Cook pasta in boiling water until tender; drain.
- Toss pasta, ½ cup feta cheese and tomato mixture together.
- Season with salt and pepper.
- Transfer pasta to serving bowl; top with remaining feta cheese.

Serves 4

Chicken and Lemon Pepper Penne

1 tablespoon butter

¾ pound boneless chicken breast, cut into pieces

3 cups broccoli florets

1 cup milk or chicken broth

¾ cup sliced carrots

½ teaspoon salt

4 cups lemon pepper penne rigate

1 (8 ounce) package cream cheese

½ cup grated Parmesan cheese

- In a large skillet, melt butter over medium heat. Add chicken and cook for 3 minutes or until no longer pink, stirring occasionally.
- Add broccoli, milk, carrots and salt; boil.
- Reduce heat to medium; cover and cook for 3 minutes or until vegetables are crisp and tender and chicken is cooked. Set aside.
- Cook pasta according to package directions; drain.
- On low heat, stir cream cheese into broccoli mixture until melted and smooth.
- Remove from heat. Stir in Parmesan cheese. Spoon sauce over hot pasta.
- Serve immediately.

Serves 6

Bowties with Cannellini Beans and Spinach

Great vegetarian dish!

8 ounces bowtie pasta
2 (10 ounce) bags spinach
1 tablespoon olive oil
1 jumbo onion, thinly sliced
2 garlic cloves, minced
1½ cups chicken broth
1½ teaspoons cornstarch
½ teaspoon crushed red pepper
1½ teaspoons basil
½ teaspoon salt
1 (15 ounce) can cannellini
   beans, drained*
½ cup freshly grated Romano or
   Parmesan cheese for topping

- Cook bowties in salted, boiling water according to package directions.
- Before draining pasta, stir spinach into the water. Leave in only until the spinach begins to wilt.
- Drain pasta and spinach; return to saucepot.
- Heat olive oil over medium-high heat in a large, non-stick skillet.
- Add onions and cook for 10 to 12 minutes or until golden brown.
- Add minced garlic to onions.
- Mix chicken broth, cornstarch, red pepper, basil, and ½ teaspoon salt together.
- Add to skillet along with beans and cook over medium-high heat for 1 minute and until sauce boils and thickens.
- Add sauce to pasta and toss.
- Top with Romano or Parmesan cheese.

Serves 4

* Variation: White kidney beans can be substituted.

Shells with Goat Cheese and Fresh Tomatoes

Great on summer evenings!

4 ripe tomatoes, chopped
4 tablespoons olive oil
½ cup chopped fresh basil
2 teaspoons salt, divided
½ teaspoon pepper
4 ounces crumbled goat cheese
1 (16 ounce) box small pasta
   shells
1 cup grated Parmesan cheese

- Mix tomatoes, olive oil, basil, 1 teaspoon salt and pepper. Set aside.
- Cook pasta in boiling, salted water for 8 minutes or until al dente.
- Drain pasta. Return to pot. Toss with tomato mixture and goat cheese.
- Top with Parmesan and serve.

Serves 4

117

Two Cheese Penne with Tomatoes and Olives

6 tablespoons olive oil, divided

¾ cup chopped onion

1 teaspoon minced garlic

3 (28 ounce) cans Italian tomatoes

1 tablespoon basil

½ teaspoon red pepper

2 cups canned chicken broth

1 pound penne

2½ cups grated Havarti cheese

⅓ cup sliced black olives

⅓ cup grated Parmesan cheese

- Heat 3 tablespoons oil in a large skillet. Add onion and garlic; sauté for 5 minutes over medium-high heat.
- Add tomatoes, basil and red pepper. Bring to a boil, breaking apart tomatoes.
- Add broth and bring to a boil. Reduce heat to low; simmer for 1 hour and until mixture thickens to a chunky sauce.
- Preheat oven to 375°.
- Cook pasta in a large pot of boiling, salted water until tender but still firm. Drain.
- Return pasta to pot; add 3 tablespoons of olive oil and toss.
- Add sauce and toss.
- Mix in Havarti cheese. Transfer pasta to a 13 x 9-inch glass baking dish. Sprinkle with olives and Parmesan.
- Bake for 30 minutes and until pasta is thoroughly heated.

Serves 8

Chicken Pasta Nests

6 angel hair pasta nests

1 (10 ounce) package frozen chopped spinach, thawed and drained

6 boneless chicken breasts

1 (4½ ounce) can of mushroom pieces, drained

1 (10¾ ounce) can cream of chicken soup

½ cup water

1 (8 ounce) package shredded cheddar cheese

- Prepare pasta nests according to package directions.
- Remove with a slotted spoon; place on paper towels to drain and cool.
- In a lightly greased 9 x 13-inch casserole dish, layer chicken breasts, pasta nests, spoonfuls of spinach and mushroom pieces.
- Dilute cream of chicken soup with ½ cup water; mix well.
- Pour over chicken nests.
- Cover and bake for 1 hour.
- Top with grated cheese the last five minutes of baking.

Serves 6

Angel Hair Pasta with Artichoke Hearts and Shrimp

8 ounces angel hair pasta

¼ cup olive oil

1 pound medium shrimp, peeled and deveined

3 cloves garlic, minced

¼ teaspoon dried crushed red pepper

1 (14 ounce) can quartered artichoke hearts, drained

1 (2¼ ounce) can sliced ripe olives

⅓ cup fresh lemon juice

⅛ teaspoon salt

⅛ teaspoon pepper

½ cup grated Parmesan cheese

- Cook pasta according to package directions. Drain; keep warm.
- Heat oil in a skillet over medium-high heat. Add shrimp, garlic and red pepper. Cook, stirring constantly for 4 to 5 minutes or until shrimp turns pink.
- Stir in artichoke hearts and next four ingredients.
- Add to pasta and sprinkle with Parmesan cheese.

Serves 4

"Don't cook what you can't pronounce."

Tomato and Vermicelli Torte

Tastes great hot or cold!

4 ounces vermicelli (break into small pieces before cooking)

1 small onion, finely chopped

2 teaspoons crushed garlic

1 tablespoon olive oil

1 teaspoon basil

1 teaspoon oregano

1 teaspoon salt

½ teaspoon pepper

¾ cup ricotta cheese

¼ cup grated Parmesan cheese

1 egg, beaten

6 ripe Roma tomatoes, thinly sliced

½ cup black olives

- Cook pasta according to package directions.
- Preheat oven to 350°.
- Sauté onions and garlic in olive oil for 5 to 7 minutes.
- Add spices.
- Mix ricotta cheese, Parmesan cheese and egg in a large bowl.
- Add pasta and garlic and onion mixture. Mix well.
- Arrange a layer of pasta in a greased, round casserole dish. Top with sliced tomatoes, repeating layers.
- Top with black olives.
- Cover and bake for 40 minutes.
- Uncover and let brown an additional 5 minutes.
- Cool before slicing.

Serves 6

Mediterranean Pasta Bake

1 (10 ounce) package mostaccioli
or penne noodles

1 (10 ounce) package frozen
chopped spinach, thawed

4 (6 ounce) boneless chicken
breasts, cut into bite-size
pieces

3 large garlic cloves, minced and
divided

1 tablespoon olive oil

1 (8 ounce) package fresh
mushrooms, sliced

1 onion, chopped

1 tablespoon butter

½ cup dry white wine

2 (14 ounce) cans whole
tomatoes with juice, chopped

3 tablespoons tomato paste

1¼ teaspoons basil

½ teaspoon fennel seed

1 teaspoon oregano

1 teaspoon salt

¾ cup grated Parmesan cheese,
divided

1 (4 ounce) package garlic and
herb feta cheese, divided

- Cook pasta according to package directions.
- Preheat oven to 350°.
- Drain spinach and set aside.
- Sauté chicken in half of the garlic and olive oil.
- In another skillet, sauté mushrooms, onions, remaining garlic, butter and wine.
- Add to chicken.
- Stir in tomatoes, tomato paste and spices. Simmer for 10 minutes.
- Stir in pasta, spinach, ½ cup Parmesan cheese, and half of feta cheese.
- Spoon mixture into a 13 x 9 x 2-inch glass baking dish.
- Sprinkle with remaining Parmesan and feta cheese.
- Bake for 25 minutes.
- Note: Try this without chicken for a great meatless dish.

Serves 8 to 10

> "The best party is a mix of people...not just ones who know each other."

Louisiana Fettuccine

Served best with hot French bread.

1½ cups chicken broth

3 cups heavy cream

½ cup plus 3 tablespoons butter, divided

1 medium onion, chopped

1 medium bell pepper, chopped

3 garlic cloves, minced

1 tablespoon minced fresh basil

1 pound andouille sausage or spicy kielbasa

2 pounds medium-size shrimp, peeled

3 tablespoons flour

½ teaspoon salt

1 teaspoon cayenne pepper

6 green onions, chopped

1 pound fettuccine

Freshly grated Parmesan cheese

- Cook pasta according to package directions. Drain.
- Bring chicken broth to a boil in a heavy saucepan.
- Add cream and simmer, reducing liquid by about half.
- Melt ½ cup butter in a deep skillet.
- Add onion, bell pepper, garlic, basil and sausage.
- Sauté until onion is clear.
- Add shrimp and cook for five minutes.
- Remove from skillet and place in a mixing bowl.
- Melt 3 tablespoons butter in the skillet.
- Add flour and cook until thickened, stirring constantly.
- Slowly add cream mixture; then add salt and pepper.
- Season to taste.
- Stir in shrimp mixture.
- Add green onions and fettuccine; heat.
- Sprinkle each serving with grated Parmesan cheese.

Serves 6 to 8

Smoked Turkey Fettuccine with Pecans

3 tablespoons unsalted butter

¼ cup diced onion

3 tablespoons diced red pepper

2 teaspoons minced garlic

1 cup whipping cream

½ cup coarsely chopped pecans, lightly toasted

¼ pound smoked turkey, cut julienne

¼ cup ricotta cheese

2 tablespoons fresh cilantro

8 ounces fettuccine

½ teaspoon salt

¼ teaspoon pepper

- Sauté onion, pepper and garlic in butter for 5 minutes.
- Add next five ingredients and bring to a boil on low heat, stirring constantly. Simmer a few additional minutes. Remove from heat. Cover pan with lid and set aside.
- Cook fettuccine according to package directions. Drain.
- Add fettuccine to sauce and heat thoroughly. Stir in salt and pepper; serve immediately.

Serves 4 to 6

Marinated Mushroom Pasta with Chicken

Serve with fresh garlic bread.

1/4 cup olive oil

1 garlic clove, minced

4 boneless chicken breasts, cut into bite-size pieces

2 tablespoons oregano

2 tablespoons soy sauce

1 cup white wine

1 bunch broccoli, cut into florets, stems discarded

1 (16 ounce) jar marinated Italian mushrooms, drained and chopped

2 pounds angel hair pasta

4 tablespoons butter, melted

1/2 cup Italian-style bread crumbs

2 cups shredded Parmesan cheese

- Heat olive oil over medium heat in a large saucepan.
- Add garlic and sauté.
- Add chicken and cook until lightly browned.
- Add oregano, soy sauce and wine. Simmer uncovered for two minutes.
- Add broccoli and cover; cook until soft.
- Add mushrooms and cover; cook two minutes.
- Remove from heat. Cover and set aside.
- Cook pasta according to package directions.
- Combine chicken and pasta.
- Toss in butter, bread crumbs and cheese.

Serves 8

Spicy Spinach Manicotti

1 (16 ounce) package manicotti shells

2 (15 ounce) containers part-skim ricotta cheese

4 cups shredded mozzarella cheese

½ cup grated Parmesan cheese

½ teaspoon salt

½ teaspoon pepper

1 (10 ounce) box frozen chopped spinach, thawed and drained

2 (26 ounce) jars spicy spaghetti sauce

1 pound hot pork sausage

- Cook manicotti shells according to package directions.
- Drain manicotti and cool.
- Preheat oven to 350°.
- Stir together ricotta cheese, mozzarella, Parmesan cheese, salt, pepper, and spinach.
- Spoon mixture into manicotti shells.
- Spread a thin layer of spaghetti sauce on the bottom of a lightly greased baking pan.
- Arrange manicotti on top of sauce.
- Pour a spoonful of sauce on the top, middle section of each manicotti.
- Cover and bake for 40 minutes.
- Uncover and bake for an additional 15 to 20 minutes.
- To make topping, brown sausage; drain. Add second jar of sauce and simmer.
- Serve sauce over manicotti.

Serves 8

"Good food, good wine, an excellent guest list. Just make it happy."

Chicken Madrid

This spicy casserole has been known to send several overdue mothers into labor!

1 medium onion, chopped

4 tablespoons butter

4 boneless chicken breast halves, cooked and chopped

1 (10¾ ounce) can cream of chicken soup

1 cup sour cream

1 cup mild or hot salsa

1 tablespoon cumin

2 tablespoons chili powder

1 tablespoon minced garlic

8 burrito-style flour tortillas, cut into 1-inch pieces

8 ounces shredded cheddar cheese or shredded Mexican taco-style cheese

- Preheat oven to 350°.
- Sauté onion in butter until tender.
- In a large bowl, combine onion, chicken, soup, sour cream, salsa, spices and garlic. Mix well.
- In a greased 9 x 13-inch baking dish, layer half of tortillas, then chicken and salsa mixture, remaining tortillas and cheese.
- Bake uncovered for 30 minutes.
- Note: Serve this casserole with Jalapeño Cornbread on page 44.

Serves 6 to 8

"I recently received a 'thank you' note for attending a lovely morning luncheon. I was so touched by the host's humility and appreciation, that I wrote her TWO thank you notes-one for the invitation, and one for her 'thank you' note! It's always nice to feel appreciated."

Shrimp, Chicken, and Artichoke Casserole

2 (14 ounce) cans artichoke
  hearts, quartered and drained

2 pounds cooked shrimp, peeled
  and deveined

6 boneless, chicken breast
  halves, cooked and chopped

2 tablespoons unsalted butter

1½ pounds mushrooms, sliced

¾ cup unsalted butter

¾ cup flour

3 cups milk, warmed

1 tablespoon Worcestershire
  sauce

½ cup sherry

Salt and pepper to taste

½ cup grated Parmesan cheese

Paprika to taste

- Preheat oven to 375°.
- Arrange artichoke hearts on the bottom of a greased 9 x 13-inch baking dish.
- Add shrimp and chicken to baking dish.
- In a small skillet, melt 2 tablespoons butter. Add mushrooms and sauté for 2 minutes. Add mushrooms to baking dish.
- In a medium saucepan, melt ¾ cup butter over low heat. Slowly blend in flour, mixing well to form a roux. Gradually add milk, stirring constantly until sauce is thick and creamy.
- Add Worcestershire sauce, sherry, salt and pepper to cream sauce.
- Pour cream sauce over entire casserole.
- Sprinkle with Parmesan cheese and paprika.
- Bake uncovered for 40 minutes.
- Note: Serve with plain white rice as this dish is quite rich.

Serves 10

"If you have limited table seating, plan a menu that your guests can easily balance on their knees."

Chicken and Spinach Puff Bravo

1 pound Mexican-flavored processed cheese, cubed

½ cup sour cream

¼ teaspoon garlic salt

2 egg yolks

2 (10 ounce) packages frozen chopped spinach, thawed and well drained

4 boneless chicken breast halves, cooked and chopped

¼ cup diced red or green pepper

½ cup sliced mushrooms

2 (8 ounce) cans refrigerated crescent rolls

- Preheat oven to 375°.
- In a 3-quart saucepan, combine cheese, sour cream and garlic salt. Stir over low heat until cheese is melted. Remove from heat.
- Beat egg yolks thoroughly. Reserve 1 tablespoon beaten egg yolk for glaze.
- Gradually stir remaining beaten egg yolks into cheese mixture.
- Add spinach, chicken, pepper and mushrooms to cheese mixture. Set aside.
- Unroll one can of crescent dough. Separate into 8 flat triangles.
- Press triangles into a greased 12-inch round baking dish or oven-proof skillet, pressing perforations together to seal.
- Spread chicken filling over dough. Unroll second can of dough. Separate into 8 flat triangles.
- Arrange flat triangles on top of chicken mixture in a circular pattern, pointed ends towards the center.
- Brush dough with reserved egg yolks.
- Bake uncovered for 35 to 40 minutes or until bubbly.

Serves 8

"Keeping things simple is always successful. Sometimes casseroles are easier than hors d'oeuvres."

Herbed Chicken Divan

This casserole is a welcomed meal for a new mother and her family.

4 boneless chicken breast halves,
  cooked and chopped

2 (10 ounce) packages frozen
  chopped broccoli, cooked and
  well drained

1 (10¾ ounce) can cream of
  chicken soup

1 (10¾ ounce) can cream of
  broccoli soup

½ cup mayonnaise

1¼ teaspoons curry powder

½ teaspoon lemon juice

2 cups shredded cheddar cheese

1 (8 ounce) package herb-
  flavored stuffing mix

3 tablespoons butter, melted

- Preheat oven to 350°.
- Mix chicken, broccoli, soups, mayonnaise, curry powder and lemon juice in a large bowl.
- Pour chicken mixture into a greased 9 x 13-inch baking dish.
- Sprinkle cheese evenly over top of casserole.
- Cover cheese with stuffing mix and drizzle with melted butter.
- Bake uncovered for 20 to 25 minutes.
- Note: Freezes well.

Serves 10 to 12

"Our best party tip?....We called everyone
that we could think of and told them to come
to a party—BUT they had to be there in
thirty minutes or less! We ended up with a
great group of people and had a ball!"

Fiesta Chicken Casserole

6 boneless chicken breast halves

1 medium onion, chopped

1 green pepper, chopped

½ cup butter or margarine

1 (10¾ ounce) can cream of mushroom soup

1 (10¾ ounce) can cream of chicken soup

1 (10½ ounce) can diced tomatoes with green chiles

1 tablespoon Worcestershire sauce

1 (8 ounce) package shredded processed cheese

1 (8 ounce) package Mexican-flavored shredded processed cheese

1 (12 ounce) package spaghetti

1 cup bread crumbs

- Boil chicken breasts in water until tender and cooked through. Reserve cooking water.
- Chop chicken into bite-sized pieces. Set aside.
- In a large skillet or Dutch oven, sauté onion and green pepper in butter.
- Add soups, tomatoes, chiles (juice included) and Worcestershire sauce to skillet. Stir to combine.
- Add cheeses and stir over low heat until cheeses are melted.
- Stir in chicken. Remove skillet from heat.
- Preheat oven to 350°.
- Boil spaghetti per package instructions in reserved water. Drain well.
- Toss spaghetti gently into chicken mixture.
- Transfer mixture to a greased 9 x 13-inch baking dish. Top evenly with bread crumbs.
- Bake uncovered for 30 to 40 minutes or until bubbly.

Serves 8 to 10

"For my parents' anniversary, family and friends were asked to bring a special memory page and picture. The pages were then made into a wonderful memory-filled scrapbook."

Grilling and Game

Harvest Thyme

Harvest Thyme

In the early 1900's, downtown Paducah was the place to be on Saturday night. During the harvest season, area farmers brought their produce to sell at the town's open air Market House. Meat producers, as well, did a brisk business from their vendor stalls. Retail stores, restaurants, and banks kept extended hours for the convenience of the vendors who, at the end of the day, had cash to save or to spend. Saturday night strolling or driving down Broadway was great entertainment. The vendors' stalls disappeared in the 1950's but the building remained intact, thanks to preservationists who proposed that it be used as a community arts center, with an historic museum, art gallery, and theatre.

Today, the Market House Square area still draws crowds, not only on Saturday night, as in the old days, but on special occasions such as Paducah's Annual Barbecue Festival. For this event, which takes place in September, amateur and professional barbecuers from all over the region test their special recipes and secret sauces, fire up their smokers, and bring out their best for the public to savor. Much like the vendors of days gone by, they set up "market stalls" of their own to display their harvest of barbecued pork, beef, and chicken. The aroma of the hickory-smoke filled air brings thousands of barbecue lovers to the downtown area looking to sample the grilled meats and partake in the fun.

At home, on our own backyard grills, we try to outdo the experts with our own versions of secret sauces. Barbecue Thyme is Harvest Thyme for our guests who enjoy our grilling efforts as well as a bounty of fresh salads and vegetables served at a late summer grill out.

Late Summer Grill Out

Chutney Cheese Spread

Outdoor Roasted Chicken

Wild Mushroom and Sausage Dressing

Deer Camp Slaw

Jalapeño Cornbread

Southern Pecan Pie

Harvest Thyme Hints:

Reap what you sow—Snip your fresh garden herbs and try the *Grilled Basil Chicken* (page 134).

Fresh, Fresh, Fresh—What a wonderful time of year to enjoy a bounty of fresh garden vegetables and herbs.

Harvest Moon—Grilling by moonlight might be romantic, but it won't get the job "done." Make sure outdoor lighting is appropriate for the grilling area.

Bourbon Wine Steaks

Simple and elegant. Great with grilled vegetables.

4 bacon slices
4 (1½- to 2-inch thick) beef filets

Marinade:
⅓ cup bourbon
1 cup dry red wine
½ cup soy sauce
2 tablespoons Worcestershire
    sauce
2 garlic cloves, minced
Cracked black pepper to taste

- Wrap bacon slices around filets and secure with tooth-picks.
- Combine marinade ingredients and marinate steaks for 1 to 2 hours.
- Grill over medium heat until desired temperature, usually 10 to 15 minutes on each side for medium filets.

Serves 4

Grilled Chicken and Shrimp

Great served with rice.

1 (1.36 ounce) package honey
    teriyaki marinade mix
1 pound boneless chicken
    breasts, cut into large cubes
1 pound medium raw shrimp,
    peeled and deveined
1 large green pepper, cut into
    large pieces
1 (20 ounce) can pineapple
    chunks, drained

- Mix marinade according to package directions.
- Place half of marinade in a bowl with the chicken and the other half in a bowl with the shrimp; marinate for at least an hour.
- Preheat grill to medium heat. Use a grill basket or a shallow foil pan. Spray with nonstick cooking spray.
- Grill chicken and green peppers until done, about 15 to 20 minutes. Remove from basket. Grill shrimp with pineapple. When shrimp is pink, add chicken and green pepper; heat through.

Serves 4 to 6

"Let your husband grill or smoke the meat. It makes entertaining so much easier and more of a group effort."

Beef Tenderloin on the Grill

Great for elegant entertaining or summer patio dining!

1 (3 to 4 pound) beef tenderloin
½ cup olive oil
Seasoned salt to taste

Gravy:
1 (10.5 ounce) can beef gravy
1 (10.5 ounce) can au jus
½ cup red wine
1 (8 ounce) package fresh
    mushrooms, sliced

- Preheat grill to medium heat.
- Trim fat from tenderloin.
- Brush meat with olive oil and generously sprinkle with seasoned salt.
- Place tenderloin on grill and close the lid. Let cook for 20 minutes without opening the lid.
- After 20 minutes, turn meat over and grill an additional 20 minutes. For rare meat, cook only 15 additional minutes.
- Remove tenderloin and slice beef onto a serving platter.
- To make gravy, combine beef gravy with au jus. Add red wine and mushrooms and simmer until heated.

Serves 6 to 8

Grilled Turkey Breast

1 (3 to 4 pound) turkey breast
4 tablespoons kosher salt
4 tablespoons olive oil
1 medium onion, cut into
    wedges
1 orange, cut into wedges
1 lemon, cut into wedges
4 garlic cloves

- Wash breast under running water. Scrub with salt and rinse. Coat with oil.
- Stuff cavity of breast with wedges of onion, orange, lemon and garlic cloves. Use 3 to 4 skewers to secure.
- Grill over medium-high grill for 1½ hours, turning every 15 minutes or until turkey timer indicates done.

Variation: This is great with a favorite chutney on the side or for the best sandwiches.

Serves 6

"A gentleman does not go near a kitchen."
Anonymous (Japanese saying)

Grilled Basil Chicken

4 chicken breast halves

Coarsely ground pepper

1 cup margarine, melted and
divided

⅓ cup plus 1 tablespoon chopped
fresh basil, divided

2 tablespoons grated Parmesan
cheese

¼ teaspoon garlic powder

¼ teaspoon salt

¼ teaspoon pepper

- Sprinkle chicken breasts generously with pepper. Combine ½ cup melted margarine and ⅓ cup basil. Brush chicken lightly with melted margarine, reserving some for grilling.

- Combine remaining margarine and basil, Parmesan cheese, garlic powder, salt and pepper. Beat at low speed until well blended and smooth; set aside.

- Grill chicken over medium heat for 8 to 10 minutes on each side, basting frequently with initial margarine.

- Spread the second margarine mixture over hot chicken; serve.

Serves 4

Marinated Chicken Breasts

6 boneless chicken breast halves

Marinade:

½ cup firmly packed brown
sugar

⅓ cup olive oil

¼ cup cider vinegar

3 garlic cloves, crushed

3 tablespoons coarse-grain
prepared mustard

1½ tablespoons lemon juice

1½ tablespoons lime juice

1½ teaspoons salt

¼ teaspoon pepper

- Place chicken breasts in a large, shallow dish. Combine marinade ingredients; stir well. Pour over chicken. Cover and refrigerate for at least 2 hours (longer for a more enhanced flavor).

- Remove chicken; discard marinade. Grill over hot coals for 8 minutes on each side.

Serves 6

"Galvanized buckets in different sizes make great containers for ice, chips, or centerpieces."

Outdoor Roasted Chicken

Great patio dinner; complement with white wine.

1 whole chicken, washed
2 tablespoons butter, divided
3 teaspoons chopped garlic,
  divided
Salt and pepper
2 teaspoons Cajun seasoning
2 tablespoons Worcestershire
  sauce
1 yellow onion, cut lengthwise
1 green bell pepper, cut
  lengthwise
1 celery stalk, cut in 3-inch
  pieces
½ cup dry white wine
1 cup water

- Place chicken in a pan. Rub 1 tablespoon butter and 1 teaspoon garlic all over top of chicken. Season cavity and outside of chicken with salt, pepper, Cajun seasoning and Worcestershire sauce.

- Stuff cavity with remaining butter, onions, peppers, celery and 2 teaspoons garlic. Tie legs together if necessary.

- Place a pan under wire rack on the left side of grill.

- Add ½ cup dry white wine and 1 cup water to pan.

- Spray grill rack with nonstick cooking spray. Place the chicken directly on the grill rack on the left side of grill. Light the right side of grill and close lid.

- Grill for 1 hour and 15 minutes on medium heat. Chicken is done when juices from the legs run clear. Check periodically while grilling and add additional water or wine to pan if needed.

Variation: Use beer (1 can) in place of wine.

Serves 4

Thyme and Again

Here's a great idea for leftovers: Prepare the Outdoor Roasted Chicken on Monday. Any leftover chicken can be taken off the bone, and frozen for future use or used the next day by substituting the chicken for turkey to prepare Smoked Chicken Fettuccine with Pecans (a variation of Smoked Turkey Fettuccine with Pecans, page 121.)

Spicy Cajun Shish Kabobs

Great with roasted new potatoes.

18 large shrimp, peeled and
  deveined

3 large boneless chicken breasts

1 pound smoked sausage or
  andouille, sliced 1-inch thick

2 green peppers, sliced
  lengthwise

2 large yellow onions, sliced in
  chunks

1 fresh zucchini, sliced ¼-inch
  thick

½ cup butter, melted

2 tablespoons Cajun seasoning

2 tablespoons Worcestershire
  sauce

½ teaspoon cracked black pepper

½ teaspoon lemon juice

- Wash, peel and devein shrimp. Wash chicken and cut into medium-size pieces (at least 2 for each kabob). Prepare sausage and vegetables as directed.

- Melt butter. In a large bowl, mix butter, Cajun seasoning, Worcestershire sauce, black pepper, lemon juice, chicken, sausage, shrimp and zucchini. Toss well.

- Spray skewers with nonstick spray. Assemble ingredients on skewers with an onion or pepper near the meat or shrimp for more flavor. Brush with remaining sauce.

- Spray grill prior to cooking. Grill 15 to 30 minutes until chicken is done.

- Note: For a spicier taste, sprinkle a little more Cajun seasoning on before serving.

Variation: Yellow squash, mushrooms or another favorite vegetable can be used in place of zucchini.

Serves 6

"My sister uses woody rosemary sprigs for skewers when grilling. It looks great and adds the wonderful flavor of rosemary. She also makes little rosemary bundles and uses them as butter brushes for fresh corn-on-the-cob."

Mexican Margarita Shrimp

1½ pounds large shrimp, peeled
  and deveined
¼ cup lime juice
¼ cup tequila
¼ cup water
¼ cup finely chopped onion
1 tablespoon olive oil
¼ teaspoon salt
Brown or white rice, cooked
Lime slices for garnish

- Place shrimp in a shallow 9 x 13-inch glass dish.
- Combine lime juice, tequila, water, onions, olive oil and salt in a bowl.
- Pour over shrimp; stir.
- Marinate, stirring occasionally, for 10 minutes.
- Remove shrimp from marinade, reserving marinade.
- Thread shrimp onto four, 15-inch skewers, running the skewer through each shrimp twice.
- Transfer marinade to a saucepan and bring to a boil.
- Reduce heat and simmer for 5 minutes. Set aside.
- Coat grill rack with nonstick cooking spray.
- Place kabobs on grill.
- Grill, turning once, 3 minutes on each side.
- Remove shrimp from skewers and arrange over rice.
- Spoon marinade over each serving.
- Garnish with lime slices.

Serves 4

Honey Glazed Pork Chops

4 center cut or butterfly pork chops

Honey Glaze:
½ cup honey
3 tablespoon Dijon mustard
1 tablespoon orange juice
¼ teaspoon dried tarragon
  leaves
2 teaspoons balsamic vinegar
½ teaspoon Worcestershire
  sauce

- Grill pork chops over medium heat for 15 to 20 minutes, brushing occasionally with glaze and turning only once.

Serves 4

Raspberry Honey Mustard Pork Tenderloin

Quick, easy and elegant.

2 pork tenderloins
¼ cup olive oil
1 teaspoon cracked black pepper
1 (10.8 ounce) jar raspberry
    honey mustard pretzel dip*

- Place tenderloins in a pan with a lip. Rub tenderloins with olive oil and cracked pepper.
- Coat tenderloins with pretzel dip. Refrigerate for at least one hour.
- Place on a medium grill; cover. Cook 30 minutes or until meat thermometer registers 170°, turning occasionally. Be careful not to burn.
- Note: Buy an extra jar of pretzel dip and serve on the side.

Variation: If the dip is not available, substitute ½ cup raspberry preserves and ¾ cup honey mustard as the marinade.

Serves 6

*Available at specialty stores

Sesame Garlic Grilled Pork Tenderloin

Easy and delicious for a picnic.

Marinade:
4 tablespoons soy sauce
2 tablespoons sesame oil
2 tablespoons brown sugar
1 tablespoon sherry
½ teaspoon honey
4 garlic cloves, minced
2 tablespoons sesame seeds
4 sliced scallions
1 (3 to 4 pound) pork tenderloin

- Mix marinade ingredients together. Marinate tenderloin overnight in the refrigerator.
- Grill over medium-high temperature for 30 to 40 minutes or until meat thermometer registers 170°.
- Slice in medallions and arrange on a plate.

Serves 6

Smoked Leg of Lamb

1 leg of lamb
2 tablespoons rosemary
3 tablespoons salt
1 tablespoon pepper
1 tablespoon dry mustard
6 finely chopped garlic cloves
Olive oil

- Debone the leg of lamb. Remove silver skin, tendons and most of the fat. Try to end up with three or four good size chunks of meat.
- Combine dry ingredients and grind to break up some of the rosemary leaves. Add garlic and enough olive oil to make a smooth paste. Coat the meat with the mixture.
- On outdoor smoker or grill, smoke the meat chunks away from the coals, or oven bake at 325° just until a thermometer registers nearly rare.
- Remove meat and wrap in foil; refrigerate. This can be done a day ahead.
- Second cooking: Refresh the rub for more flavor. Place the chunks of partially cooked meat over very hot coals and cook with the same method you would use for a thick steak. Monitor carefully and remove when the thermometer registers rare to medium rare.
- Slice and serve.

Serves 4 to 6

Teriyaki Mahi-Mahi

4 mahi-mahi fillets, 6 inches
    long, skinned
1 cup soy sauce
1 cup teriyaki marinade sauce,
    divided
4 fresh limes, juiced
½ cup lightly-salted butter
    (no substitutions)
½ cup orange blossom honey

- Marinate mahi-mahi fillets in ½ cup soy sauce, ½ cup teriyaki sauce and half of the lime juice for 2 hours in a ziplock bag. A ziplock bag works great.
- Create basting sauce by melting butter, honey, remaining soy and teriyaki sauces, and lime juice in a pan over low heat.
- Spray grill with nonstick cooking spray. Grill mahi-mahi fillets slowly over medium heat for 7 to 10 minutes per side. Brush basting sauce frequently over fillets. Use caution when turning.

Variation: Other white fish can be substituted for mahi-mahi.

Serves 4

Salmon on the Grill

¾ cup pecan halves

3 tablespoons honey

3 tablespoons freshly squeezed
lemon juice

½ teaspoon crushed red pepper
flakes

2 tablespoons olive oil

3 fresh garlic cloves, minced

1 side fresh Atlantic salmon
(6 ounces per person)

Salt and pepper to taste

- Preheat oven to 350°.
- Scatter the pecan halves in a baking pan and toast in oven until nuts are fragrant, about 10 minutes. Shake pan occasionally while toasting.
- Finely chop the pecans and combine them in a small bowl with honey, lemon juice and red pepper flakes, mixing well.
- Heat grill to 400° to 450°.
- Mix olive oil and garlic in a small container.
- Brush flesh side of salmon with garlic oil.
- Place salmon, flesh side down, on the grill. Grill five minutes, then turn.
- Sprinkle flesh side with salt and pepper, then spread the top with pecan mixture. Close grill lid and grill for another 7 minutes or until fish flakes easily.
- Serve on a bed of baby salad greens.

Serves 6

Creole Grilled Tuna

½ cup butter, melted

1 tablespoon Worcestershire
sauce

1 teaspoon Creole seasoning

½ lemon, juiced

4 (10 ounce) tuna steaks,
1-inch thick

- Mix butter, Worcestershire sauce, Creole seasoning and lemon juice in a small bowl. Brush onto tuna steaks; cover and refrigerate for 30 minutes.
- Spray wire rack with nonstick cooking spray. Heat grill to high.
- Grill tuna for 2 to 3 minutes on each side, or less time for rare steaks. Be careful not to tear the tuna steaks when removing from the grill.
- Serve hot.

Olive oil (½ cup) can be substituted for butter. Try adding a few drops of Tabasco sauce to the marinade.

Serves 4

Seasoned Grilled Potatoes

Great with grilled pork!

2 pounds new potatoes, washed
½ cup margarine or butter, melted
2 garlic cloves, minced
1 teaspoon seasoned salt
Pepper to taste

- Heat grill to medium.
- Cut the larger potatoes in half or quarters for uniform pieces.
- Combine margarine, garlic and salt.
- Pour mixture over potatoes and place in an 8-inch square foil pan or on a large sheet of heavy-duty foil. Season with pepper.
- Cover pan with foil or seal foil packet allowing room for expansion.
- Place potatoes on grill. Cook for 35 to 45 minutes or until potatoes are tender.
- Stir potatoes several times during cooking.

Variation: Add 2 tablespoons chopped, fresh herbs. Olive oil can be substituted for butter.

Serves 8

Pheasant with Wine Sauce

2 pheasants, split
½ cup water
1 teaspoon salt
⅛ teaspoon pepper
1 onion, finely chopped
2 cups sliced fresh mushrooms
½ cup butter
2 cups dry white wine
2 tablespoons lemon juice
½ cup chopped green onions

- Place pheasant in a Dutch oven. Add water, salt, pepper and onion. Cook over medium heat for 15 minutes.
- Meanwhile, sauté mushrooms in butter. Add wine, lemon juice and green onions. Pour mixture over pheasant.
- Cover and simmer over low heat for 2 hours.
- Note: Serve with white rice.

Serves 4

Spicy Pheasant

1 pound Italian sausage, cut into
    bite-size pieces

2 tablespoons butter

2 pheasants, cut into large pieces

1 (16 ounce) can tomato purée

1 (4 ounce) can button
    mushrooms or ½ cup sliced
    fresh mushrooms

1 (10.5 ounce) can pitted ripe
    olives

¼ cup liquid drained from olives

1½ teaspoons celery flakes

1 tablespoon chopped fresh
    parsley

1½ teaspoons Italian seasoning

1 teaspoon instant onion

½ teaspoon salt

½ teaspoon pepper

¼ teaspoon garlic salt

1 bay leaf

- Brown sausage pieces in a large Dutch oven. Remove sausage and set aside. Discard grease.
- Melt butter in Dutch oven. Add pheasant pieces and sauté until brown. Remove pheasant and set aside.
- Add tomato purée and remaining ingredients to Dutch oven, stirring well.
- Return sausage and pheasant to pot and stir gently.
- Cover pot and simmer for 1½ hours or until pheasant is tender.

Serves 6

Venison Steak à la Panther Creek Lodge

4 venison steaks or chops

¼ teaspoon Tabasco sauce

1 tablespoon Worcestershire
    sauce

¼ cup soy sauce

1 tablespoon oil

1 teaspoon Dijon mustard

Juice of one lemon

- Place steaks side by side in a glass dish; set aside.
- Combine remaining ingredients in a small saucepan. Over low heat, stir marinade until heated through.
- Pour marinade over steaks. Cover dish and allow to stand at room temperature for several hours, turning occasionally.
- Grill steaks over hot coals.

Serves 4

After the Hunt Quail Dinner

12 quail, split in half

1 cup dry red wine

¼ cup red wine vinegar

¾ cup cane syrup or dark syrup

3 tablespoons minced garlic

1 tablespoon dried thyme

1 tablespoon dried basil

1 tablespoon chopped fresh
   rosemary

Salt and pepper to taste

2 tablespoons Creole seasoning

2 tablespoons Worcestershire
   sauce

1 tablespoon honey mustard

- Place quail in a baking dish; set aside.
- To prepare marinade, combine remaining ingredients. Pour mixture over quail. Rub mixture thoroughly into quail.
- Cover and refrigerate for 30 minutes.
- Preheat grill.
- Place quail, bone side down, over hot coals and grill for 5 minutes.
- Turn quail and grill for an additional 3 minutes, taking caution not to burn.
- Use additional marinade for basting, adding more Worcestershire sauce if necessary.
- Note: Wild rice is the perfect accompaniment to quail.

Variation: Quail may also be dipped in hot, spicy mustard as an alternative appetizer.

Serves 6

"For outside barbecues and picnics, try large washcloths or dishtowels in festive colors instead of regular napkins. They are more absorbent and are easily thrown in the wash for use again and again."

Duck and Dressing

2 cups finely cubed cornbread
  stuffing, toasted
2 cups finely cubed bread
  stuffing, toasted
⅓ cup butter
¼ cup finely chopped onion
½ cup finely chopped celery and
  leaves
1 teaspoon salt
⅛ teaspoon pepper
1 teaspoon sage
1 teaspoon thyme
1 teaspoon margarine
Poultry season to taste
2 cans chicken broth, divided
1-2 duck breasts

- Combine toasted bread and cornbread stuffing.
- In a heavy skillet, melt butter. Add onions and celery; sauté until tender.
- Stir in stuffing. Heat and stir often.
- Add salt, pepper, sage, thyme, margarine and poultry seasoning; moisten with 1 can of chicken broth.
- Boil duck breasts in water until tender. Shred or finely chop duck.
- Preheat oven to 250°.
- Mix duck in with stuffing mixture.
- Place in a 9 x 13-inch casserole dish. Add second can of chicken broth to wet the mixture. Cover and bake for 2 hours.

Variation: This also can be made with goose.

Serves 10

"One Christmas party I went to allowed the couples to take their beautiful Christmas tree embossed wine glasses home. Now my husband and I have a pair of glasses that remind us of that lovely evening."

Vegetables and Sides

Half Thyme

Half Thyme

Kentuckians are enthusiastic sports fans. Here in our town, we fill school stadiums and gyms to cheer our youngsters to victory. We love our collegiate sports, too, and tickets to college games are coveted prizes. Even more treasured are the hard-to-get tickets to SEC and NCAA tournament games.

For those of us unable to secure seats on the 50-yard line or at center court, home-viewing proves to be a desirable substitute. On these occasions, friends gather to watch the action. There are many advantages to this mode of game-watching. There are no parking problems, crowds, or hard seats. Wide-screen viewing is infinitely superior to the distraction of the over-excited fan in front of you, on his feet and waving a pompon. If we sports experts doubt a referee's call, there's always instant replay to confirm our opinions.

At a home-viewing party, we don't have to settle for overpriced hot dogs and drinks. Instead, we celebrate the kick-off or tip-off with beverages and hors d'oeuvres. And at half-time, there is a spread of delicious food, usually a potluck buffet provided by the guests. There might be ham, barbecue, or chicken, with sides of vegetable casseroles and salads.

Pre-game celebrations are another way to cheer on favorite teams. Tailgating, even for high school games, is as much fun for the food and fellowship as it is for the sports action. Fans show their spirit by decorating their cars, waving pennants, and dressing in their team's colors. One can expect to see everything from picnic baskets to an elaborate layout of food complete with table linens and cloth napkins. And of course, no tailgating party in our region would be complete without some version of a layered taco dip (try our Spicy Taco Dip, page 26).

No matter the team or its record, Kentuckians enjoy Half Thyme every time!

Tailgate Party

Sweet Bourbon Slush

Spicy Taco Dip

Antipasto Appetizer

Crab and Cheese Pirogue

Green Chile Pie

Party Cheese Straws

Monday's Red Beans and Rice

Incredible Edibles

Half Thyme:

Kick Off Your Celebration—with a toast, the team's fight song, or a simple hip, hip, hooray!

Catch the Spirit—by placing flowers in a megaphone, or pennants on the tailgate, or old letter sweaters as chair covers.

Tailgating—means travel, but not without taste. Prepare a menu that will hold up in a parking lot or dusty field.

Lemon Vinaigrette Asparagus

1 pound fresh asparagus
4 tablespoons pine nuts, toasted
¼ cup olive oil
1 tablespoon fresh lemon juice
1 garlic clove, minced
½ teaspoon oregano
1 teaspoon basil
Salt and pepper to taste

- Steam asparagus for approximately 10 minutes (do not overcook).
- Toast pine nuts.
- Whisk remaining ingredients together to make vinaigrette.
- Heat in a saucepan until warm but not to boiling.
- Drain asparagus and toss with vinaigrette.
- Garnish with pine nuts.

Serves 4 to 6

Asparagus Wraps

Easy and delicious!

2 tablespoons butter
2 tablespoons flour
½ teaspoon dry mustard
1 cup milk
12 fresh asparagus spears
4 slices Virginia baked ham,
    thinly sliced
½ cup grated cheddar cheese

- Preheat oven to 350°.
- Melt butter in saucepan.
- Add flour and mustard, stirring until smooth.
- Slowly add milk and cook until thick and bubbly.
- Remove from heat.
- Wrap 3 asparagus spears with a slice of ham and secure with a toothpick. Repeat.
- Place wraps in a 9 x 9-inch baking dish.
- Pour sauce over wraps.
- Bake for 20 minutes. Sprinkle cheddar cheese over hot wraps.

Serves 4

One cannot think well, love well, sleep well, if one has not dined well."
    Virginia Woolf, "A Room of One's Own," 1929

Marinated Green Beans and Artichokes

Marinade:

1½ cups sugar

2 cups oil

1 cup apple cider vinegar

2 garlic cloves, chopped

1 teaspoon salt

4 (14.5 ounce) cans cut green
  beans (preferably Italian)

2 (14 ounce) cans artichoke
  hearts, drained and cut

- Mix the marinade with a beater. Pour over beans and artichokes.
- Refrigerate for 24 hours.
- Heat for 20 to 25 minutes in a 300° oven or serve cold.
- Note: This recipe can be halved.

Serves 8 to 10

Toasted Sesame Broccoli

1 bunch broccoli

2 tablespoons sesame seeds,
  toasted

2 tablespoons oil

3 tablespoons red wine vinegar

2 tablespoons soy sauce

2 teaspoons sugar

- Steam broccoli to desired tenderness.
- While broccoli is steaming, toast sesame seeds.
- Mix remaining ingredients together and heat.
- Pour sauce over broccoli just before serving.
- Top with toasted sesame seeds.

Serves 4

Roasted Asparagus Parmesan

Makes a great presentation!

2 pounds fresh asparagus,
  trimmed

2 tablespoons olive oil

 Pinch of salt

½ cup freshly grated Parmesan
  cheese

¼ teaspoon pepper

- Preheat oven to 400°.
- Arrange asparagus on a jelly-roll pan.
- Toss with olive oil and salt.
- Roast 15 minutes on middle oven rack.
- Sprinkle with cheese and pepper.

Serves 6 to 8

Broccoli Divine

1 bunch fresh broccoli
⅓ cup finely chopped green
   onion
1 garlic clove, minced
½ teaspoon dry mustard
½ teaspoon thyme
¼ cup olive oil
3 tablespoon balsamic vinegar
1 teaspoon Dijon mustard
 Salt and pepper to taste

- Steam broccoli.
- Combine green onions, garlic, dry mustard and thyme in a bowl. Set aside.
- Heat oil in a saucepan until hot.
- Pour hot oil over green onions; stir.
- Whisk in vinegar, Dijon mustard, salt and pepper to make vinaigrette.
- Pour warm vinaigrette over broccoli and toss.

Serves 6

Green Bean Bundles

Great for a dinner buffet!

½ cup butter
¾ cup firmly packed brown
   sugar
2 teaspoons garlic powder
3 (14.5 ounce) cans whole green
   beans
15-18 bacon slices, slightly
   cooked and cut in half

- Preheat oven to 350°.
- Melt butter, sugar and garlic to make a paste.
- Gather 6 to 8 green beans for each bundle.
- Wrap each bundle with ½ slice bacon and secure with toothpicks.
- Top each bundle with equal amounts of paste.
- Place in a 9 x 13-inch baking dish.
- Bake for 20 minutes.

Serves 8

"Keeping the cold things cold and the hot things hot are the greatest challenges for any tailgating party. Bring as many ice packs that will fit in the cooler, and before leaving your home, try heating some clay trivets or bread stones in the oven. Then wrap them in dish towels and place on your tailgate under your casseroles and/or meat trays."

Buffet Green Beans

8 bacon slices
1 large onion, sliced
½ cup white vinegar
¼ cup sugar
3 (14.5 ounce) cans French-style
  green beans, drained

- Cook bacon and onion in a large skillet.
- Remove bacon and onion with a slotted spoon, reserving ¼ cup drippings in pan.
- Drain bacon and onion on a paper towel; set aside.
- Combine vinegar and sugar.
- Pour vinegar mixture into reserved drippings and bring to a boil.
- Add beans and cook over medium heat until thoroughly heated, stirring occasionally.
- Spoon into serving dish.
- Top with crumbled bacon and onions.

Serves 6 to 8

"When we tailgate, my husband insists on bringing the portable radio. To him, pre-game interviews are just as important as the pre-game hors d'oeuvres."

Famous Baked Beans

Great for a crowd!

1 pound ground chuck
1 large onion, chopped
1 green pepper, chopped
3 (15 ounce) cans pork and beans
½ cup firmly packed light brown
  sugar
½ cup firmly packed dark brown
  sugar
1 (14 ounce) bottle ketchup
2 tablespoons mustard
1 dash Worcestershire sauce

- Preheat oven to 350°.
- Brown ground chuck, onions and green peppers together; drain.
- Add remaining ingredients.
- Mix well and pour into a 3-quart greased casserole dish.
- Bake for 1 hour.

Serves 10

Fresh Green Beans with Feta

This is delicious served chilled or warm.

1½ pounds fresh green beans

Dressing:
1 tablespoon white wine vinegar
1½ tablespoons fresh lemon juice
1 teaspoon Dijon mustard
½ teaspoon dried basil
1 teaspoon sugar
Salt and pepper to taste
⅓ cup olive oil

Garnish:
¾ cup chopped red onion
½ cup crumbled feta cheese
½ cup chopped walnuts, toasted

- Cook beans in boiling water for 5 minutes or until tender.
- Prepare a large bowl of ice water.
- Drain beans and plunge into water.
- Drain again and pat dry with a paper towel.
- To make dressing, combine all ingredients except olive oil.
- Slowly whisk in olive oil until thickened.
- Place beans in a serving dish and drizzle dressing over them.
- Top with onion, feta and walnuts.
- Serve immediately or cover and chill.

Serves 4

Corn Soufflé

1 (16 ounce) can cream style corn
1 (16 ounce) can whole corn, drained
¼ cup sugar
1 cup butter-flavored cracker crumbs
2 tablespoons margarine
3 eggs, beaten
Salt and pepper

- Preheat oven to 350°.
- Mix all ingredients and pour into a greased soufflé dish or a 2-quart baking dish.
- Bake for 30 to 40 minutes or until center is firm.

Variation: May substitute 2 cups fresh corn scraped from the cob for the 16 ounce can whole corn.

Serves 6 to 8

"Hospitality is a form of worship."

Jewish proverb

Baked Four-Bean Casserole

Delicious variation of baked beans!

1 (16 ounce) can kidney beans,
   drained
1 (15.25 ounce) can green lima
   beans, drained
1 (16 ounce) can white butter
   beans, drained
3 (15.5 ounce) cans pork and beans
½ pound bacon
2 large onions, chopped
1 cup firmly packed brown
   sugar

- Preheat oven to 350°.
- Combine beans in a large bowl.
- Fry bacon. Remove bacon from skillet. Drain on paper towels and crumble bacon.
- Sauté onions in drippings.
- Mix bacon, onions and brown sugar with beans.
- Pour into a 2-quart greased casserole.
- Bake for 1 hour.

Serves 12

Monday's Red Beans and Rice

Garlic cheese bread makes this meal even better!

1 pound dried kidney beans
½ cup olive oil
1 large yellow onion, chopped
1 large green pepper, chopped
3 celery stalks, chopped
3 fresh garlic cloves, chopped
1 cup green onions (reserve some
   for garnish)
1½ pounds andouille or smoked
   sausage, sliced ½-inch thick
1 (10 ounce) can diced tomatoes
   with green chiles
½ cup chopped fresh parsley
4 bay leaves
2 tablespoons Worcestershire sauce
 Salt and pepper to taste
3 dashes hot sauce
2 cups white rice, cooked

- Rinse and soak beans in 4 quarts of water overnight or several hours before cooking.
- Heat oil on medium heat in a large stock pot.
- Add onion, green pepper, celery and garlic. Sauté for five minutes.
- Add green onions and sausage. Sauté until sausage is brown.
- Drain beans and add to stock pot. Blend well. Cook for two minutes, then add tomatoes, parsley, bay leaves, Worcestershire sauce, salt, pepper and hot sauce.
- Add enough water to cover beans (approximately 3 quarts).
- Bring to a boil and cook for 30 minutes, being careful not to burn.
- Reduce heat to low and simmer for 1 hour or until beans are soft. Stir occasionally.
- Serve with cooked rice and garnish with green onions.

Serves 6

Pineapple Cheese Casserole

3 (20 ounce) cans pineapple
    chunks (reserve 9 tablespoons
    juice)
1½ cups sugar
9 tablespoons flour
3 cups shredded cheddar cheese
¾ cup margarine, melted
1½ cups butter-flavored cracker
    crumbs

- Preheat oven to 350°.
- Drain pineapple, reserving 9 tablespoons of juice.
- Combine sugar, flour and pineapple juice.
- Add pineapple chunks and cheese.
- Pour into a lightly sprayed 9 x 13-inch pan.
- Combine melted margarine and cracker crumbs, mixing well.
- Spoon over pineapple dish.
- Bake for 20 minutes.

Serves 8 to 10

Carrots in Vermouth

2 pounds carrots, thinly sliced
2 medium celery stalks, finely diced
1 small onion, minced
½ cup sugar
2 tablespoons butter
¾ cup vermouth

- Combine all ingredients in a saucepan; cook over low heat for approximately 20 minutes or until just tender.

Serves 6

Gourmet Carrots

Easy and colorful!

2 pounds carrots, peeled and sliced
½ cup butter
⅓ cup finely chopped onion
⅓ cup chopped fresh parsley

- Bring carrots to a boil in lightly salted water.
- Cook for 10 to 15 minutes or until tender; drain. Set aside.
- Sauté butter and onions for 2 minutes.
- Add carrots and toss well.
- Sprinkle with parsley and mix well.
- Serve warm.

Serves 8

Squash Casserole Supreme

8 small squash, sliced
2 large onions
¼ cup butter
1 teaspoon beef bouillon
    granules
1 (8 ounce) container sour
    cream
1 egg, beaten
 Salt and pepper to taste
½ teaspoon sugar

- Boil squash and onions together for 20 minutes; drain.
- In the same pan, add butter, bouillon, sour cream, egg, salt and pepper.
- Mash together. Pour in a 2-quart greased casserole dish. Sprinkle with sugar.
- Bake at 350° for 30 minutes.

Serves 6 to 8

Spinach and Artichoke Casserole

2 (10 ounce) packages frozen
    spinach
1 (14 ounce) can artichoke
    hearts, chopped
1 (8 ounce) can sliced water
    chestnuts
½ cup butter
2 (8 ounce) packages cream
    cheese
2½ tablespoons chopped green
    onion
1 garlic clove, minced
1 teaspoon pepper
⅛ teaspoon salt
 Dash of red pepper
1 cup butter-flavored cracker
    crumbs

- Preheat oven to 350°.
- Cook spinach and drain well.
- Butter a 9 x 13-inch casserole dish.
- Place artichoke hearts in bottom of casserole dish.
- Layer with water chestnuts.
- Melt butter and cream cheese over low heat in a double boiler.
- Add spinach to melted cream cheese.
- Stir in onions, garlic and seasonings.
- Pour over water chestnuts; sprinkle with cracker crumbs.
- Bake for 35 minutes.

Serves 6

Sweet, Sweet Potato Casserole

Perfect for Thanksgiving dinner!

3 cups cooked and mashed sweet
   potatoes
½ cup sugar
½ cup firmly packed light brown
   sugar
½ teaspoon salt
2 eggs, beaten
3 tablespoons butter or
   margarine, melted
½ cup evaporated milk
1½ teaspoons vanilla

Topping:
1 cup firmly packed light brown
   sugar
⅓ cup flour
1 cup chopped pecans
⅓ cup butter or margarine,
   melted

- Preheat oven to 350°.
- Mix all ingredients with mashed sweet potatoes.
- Put in a 2-quart casserole dish.
- Prepare topping by mixing all ingredients; sprinkle on top of potatoes.
- Bake for 35 to 40 minutes.

Serves 10 to 12

Company Wild Rice

1 (10¾ ounce) can consommé
1 (10¾ ounce) can cream of
   mushroom soup
1 (10¾ ounce) can French onion
   soup
¾ cup wild rice
¼ cup white rice
½ cup margarine

- Preheat oven to 350°.
- Mix together all soups.
- Cut margarine into small pieces and add to soup.
- Add rice and put in a 2½-quart casserole dish.
- Place casserole dish in a pan of water and bake for 1 hour 45 minutes.

Serves 8

Potatoes Lyonnaise

Everyone will love these!

2½ pounds red potatoes, unpeeled

2 tablespoons butter or margarine

½ cup chopped green onion

⅓ cup chopped red pepper

2 garlic cloves, minced

¼ teaspoon ground red cayenne pepper

2 cups whipping cream

¾ cup milk

¾ teaspoon salt

¼ teaspoon fresh ground pepper

2 cups shredded Swiss cheese or Gruyère

¼ cup Parmesan cheese

- Preheat oven to 350°.
- Cut potatoes into ⅛-inch slices; set aside.
- Melt butter over medium-high heat in a Dutch oven.
- Add onions, red pepper, garlic and cayenne pepper. Cook for two minutes.
- Add whipping cream, milk, salt and black pepper. Stir well.
- Add potato slices and bring to a boil over medium heat. Cook and stir gently for 15 minutes or until potato slices are tender.
- Spoon into a lightly greased 11 x 7 x 1½-inch baking dish.
- Sprinkle with cheeses.
- Bake for 30 to 45 minutes or until bubbly and golden brown.

Serves 8

Cheddar Mashed Potatoes

Easy to make and tastes great!

9 medium baking potatoes

1½ cups shredded cheddar cheese

1 cup heavy whipping cream

⅔ cup warm milk

½ cup butter

1 (3 ounce) package cream cheese

1½ teaspoons salt

¼ teaspoon pepper

- Wash and peel potatoes.
- Boil until tender; drain.
- Preheat oven to 350°.
- Mash potatoes. Mix in all ingredients.
- Spoon into a 9 x 11-inch baking dish.
- Bake for 25 minutes.

Serves 10

Sausage Stuffed Potatoes

Fix with a salad for a complete meal!

4 (8 ounce) Idaho potatoes,
   scrubbed and patted dry
2 tablespoons olive oil
4 sweet Italian sausages, casings
   removed
1 cup diced onion
2 tablespoons chopped fresh
   Italian (flat leaf) parsley
6 tablespoons whipping cream
¼ cup sour cream
2 egg yolks
 Salt and freshly ground pepper

- Preheat oven to 375°.
- Prick potatoes and bake for 1¼ hours.
- Heat oil in skillet. Add sausage and cook over medium heat until browned, breaking it apart as it cooks.
- Use a slotted spoon and transfer sausage to a mixing bowl.
- Add onion; toss in parsley. Set aside.
- Remove potatoes from oven; set aside to cool.
- Once cool, cut an oval section of skin off the top and scoop out the pulp, leaving a shell.
- Set shells aside and place pulp in another mixing bowl.
- Mash pulp; add whipping cream, sour cream, egg yolks, salt and pepper. Gently stir in sausage mixture.
- Stuff shells forming into mounds.
- Bake on baking sheet for an additional 15 minutes.

Serves 4

Roasted Rosemary New Potatoes

2 pounds new potatoes, scrubbed
   and quartered
1 tablespoon olive oil
2 garlic cloves, minced
2 teaspoons snipped fresh
   rosemary, or ½ teaspoon
   crushed dried rosemary
2 teaspoons snipped fresh thyme
   or ½ teaspoon crushed dried
   thyme
¼ teaspoon salt
¼ teaspoon pepper

- Preheat oven to 450°.
- Grease a 13 x 9-inch baking dish and arrange raw potatoes in dish.
- Mix oil, garlic, rosemary, thyme, salt and pepper together in a bowl.
- Pour over potatoes and toss to coat.
- Bake uncovered for 20 to 25 minutes or until tender and brown.

Serves 8

Pine Nut Rice

⅓ cup pine nuts

2 tablespoons margarine

¾ cup chopped onion

2 medium garlic cloves, minced

1 cup white rice, uncooked

2 cups chicken broth

2 tablespoons chopped fresh
    parsley

- Sauté pine nuts over low heat in a small, dry skillet for 2 to 3 minutes or until golden; set nuts aside.
- Melt margarine over medium heat in a saucepan.
- Add onion and cook for 4 to 5 minutes or until soft but not brown.
- Add garlic and cook another 2 minutes.
- Add rice and mix well.
- Add chicken broth and bring to a boil. Cover and reduce heat.
- Simmer for 16 to 20 minutes or until rice is tender.
- Stir in parsley and pine nuts.
- Serve immediately.

Serves 4

Brown Curried Rice

1 cup brown rice

2 cups water

1 chicken bouillon cube

1 tablespoon chopped fresh
    parsley

3 teaspoons fresh ground pepper

1 (14 ounce) can artichoke
    hearts, drained and chopped

½ cup light mayonnaise

1 (10 ounce) can black olives,
    chopped

1 teaspoon curry powder

1 teaspoon sherry pepper sauce

- Mix rice, water, bouillon, parsley and pepper together in a saucepan.
- Simmer for 45 minutes.
- Allow rice to cool.
- Stir in artichokes, mayonnaise, olives, curry powder and pepper sauce.
- Note: Serve room temperature or chilled.

Serves 6

Summertime Tomatoes

When tomatoes are in abundance, this is the perfect addition to the dinner table!

4 large ripe tomatoes
Salt and pepper

Topping:
4 ounces crumbled feta cheese
½ cup sliced black olives
½ cup chopped fresh basil
Olive oil to taste
Balsamic vinegar to taste

- Wash and dry tomatoes. Slice into large rounds.
- Arrange tomatoes on a platter. Season with salt and pepper.
- Top with cheese and black olives.
- Sprinkle with basil.
- Drizzle olive oil and/or balsamic vinegar over tomatoes.

Can use sliced, fresh mozzarella cheese in place of feta cheese.

Serves 4

Mushroom Casserole

½ cup butter, divided
1 pound fresh mushrooms,
  chopped
1 small onion, chopped
1 medium green pepper, chopped
1 (10½ ounce) can cream of
  mushroom soup
1 cup mayonnaise
6 bread slices
1½ cups grated cheddar cheese,
  divided
2 eggs
1 soup can of milk
2 tablespoons butter, melted for
  topping
1 cup bread crumbs for topping

- Melt ¼ cup butter in a large skillet. Add mushrooms and cook for 2 minutes.
- Add onion and green pepper; sauté for 3 minutes.
- Remove from heat. Stir in soup and mayonnaise.
- Spread ¼ cup butter on bread slices; cut into 1-inch squares.
- Layer half of the bread squares in a 9-inch baking dish. Cover with half of the mushroom mixture and ⅓ of the cheddar cheese. Repeat.
- Beat eggs and milk together; pour over casserole.
- Refrigerate for 1 hour.
- Preheat oven to 325°.
- To make topping, melt butter and toss into bread crumbs. (It may be necessary to add additional butter.)
- Top casserole with buttered bread crumbs and remaining ⅓ of cheese.
- Bake for 1 hour.

Serves 6

Wild Mushroom and Sausage Dressing

½ pound pork sausage

½ cup butter or margarine

2½ pounds assorted mushrooms
   (shiitake, portobello, etc.)

1 large onion, halved and sliced

1 bunch green onions, chopped

¼ teaspoon garlic powder

1 (10.5 ounce) can chicken broth

3 bread slices, toasted and cubed

1 (8 ounce) package herb
   stuffing mix

½ teaspoon salt

½ teaspoon pepper

1 teaspoon dried sage

1 teaspoon dried rosemary

1 teaspoon dried thyme

- Preheat oven to 375°.
- Brown sausage in a large skillet, breaking it apart as it cooks.
- Drain sausage and set aside.
- Melt butter in skillet.
- Add mushrooms, onions, and garlic powder; sauté until tender.
- Stir in sausage, broth, cubed bread, stuffing mix and seasonings.
- Place in a lightly greased 13 x 9-inch baking dish.
- Bake for 45 minutes or until lightly browned.

Serves 8 to 10

Marinated Petite Vegetables

1 cup sugar

¾ cup vinegar

1 tablespoon water

⅓ cup oil

1 teaspoon salt

1 teaspoon pepper

1 (14½ ounce) can French-style
   green beans

1 (15 ounce) can small English peas

1 (7 ounce) can shoe-peg corn

1 (2 ounce) jar pimentos, chopped

½ cup Vidalia onion, finely chopped

½ cup green onion, finely chopped

1 cup celery, chopped

- Mix sugar, vinegar, water, oil, salt and pepper. Bring to a boil; cool.
- Drain vegetables well and mix together.
- Pour liquid over vegetables; cover tightly and let season in refrigerator for 24 hours.

Serves 12

Tomato Slices with Blue Cheese

Great and easy!

4 large ripe tomatoes

1 (8 ounce) package cream
   cheese, softened

4 ounces blue cheese

2 tablespoons fresh lemon juice

3 tablespoons sour cream

4 green onions, minced

 Parsley sprigs

- Wash and dry tomatoes. Slice into large rounds.
- Mix cream cheese and blue cheese with lemon juice, sour cream and green onions.
- Spread thinly on each tomato.
- Garnish with parsley and serve.
- Note: Arrange tomatoes on lettuce leaves for a nice presentation.

Serves 4

Glorified Stuffed Tomatoes

Excellent with grilled pork tenderloin or fish!

3 large tomatoes

 Creole seasoning

1 (6 ounce) jar marinated
   artichoke hearts, chopped

1 (10 ounce) package frozen
   chopped spinach, drained

3 ounces cream cheese, softened

1 tablespoon butter

2 tablespoons sour cream

1 tablespoon chopped fresh
   oregano

1 cup grated Parmesan cheese

1 bunch green onion, chopped

2 tablespoons butter for topping

½ cup bread crumbs for topping

- Preheat oven to 350°.
- Wash and dry tomatoes; slice into halves.
- Scoop out tomato pulp (reserve pulp from two tomatoes).
- Sprinkle inside of tomatoes with Creole seasoning.
- Place in a 9 x 13-inch baking dish.
- Drain and chop artichoke hearts.
- Pat spinach dry.
- Whip cream cheese, butter, sour cream, oregano and Parmesan cheese together in a large bowl.
- Add artichokes, spinach, tomato pulp and green onions; mix well.
- Stuff tomatoes carefully with mixture.
- Melt butter and toss into bread crumbs. Top stuffed tomatoes.
- Bake for 10 to 15 minutes, making sure not to overcook.

Variation: To make into a main meal, sauté some fresh shrimp in butter. Season and chop; add to stuffing.

Serves 6

Zucchini and Tomatoes with Fresh Parmesan

Great for a summer side dish!

½ cup olive oil
3 garlic cloves, chopped
1 large yellow onion, chopped
4 green onions, chopped
1 teaspoon fresh (or dried) oregano
1 tablespoon fresh (or dried) basil
3 medium fresh zucchini, peeled
   and sliced
6 fresh Roma tomatoes, peeled and
   chopped (or 2 cans diced tomatoes)
 Salt and pepper to taste
1 cup freshly grated Parmesan
   cheese

- Heat olive oil on low heat in a large skillet.
- Add garlic and onions; sauté for 2 minutes.
- Toss oregano, basil, zucchini, tomatoes, salt and pepper together in a bowl. Add to skillet.
- Cook on low 20 to 30 minutes or until zucchini is tender.
- Toss in fresh Parmesan cheese prior to serving, allowing some for garnish.

Serves 6

Marinated Summer Vegetables

1 cauliflower head
1 bunch broccoli
1 pound mushrooms
1 (2½ ounce) jar green olives
1 (14½ ounce) can black olives
1 (14 ounce) can artichoke hearts
1 medium cucumber
1 pint cherry tomatoes

Dressing:
1 tablespoon seasoned salt
1 tablespoon dill weed
1 teaspoon salt
1 teaspoon pepper
1 teaspoon garlic salt
1½ cups vegetable oil
1 cup vinegar
1 tablespoon sugar
½ cup Italian dressing

- Separate cauliflower and broccoli into bite-size pieces.
- Add mushrooms, olives and artichoke hearts.
- Mix dressing ingredients and pour over vegetables. Marinate overnight.
- Add cucumbers and cherry tomatoes the last four hours.

Serves 6 to 8

Autumn Medley

This will receive a lot of compliments!

⅔ teaspoon dried rosemary, plus two pinches, divided

2 teaspoons sugar

2 teaspoons salt, divided

½ teaspoon pepper, divided

2 cups peeled and sliced Granny Smith apples

1 cup peeled and sliced pears (firm)

1 cup canned, sliced carrots

1 cup canned, cut green beans

1 cup canned navy or great northern beans, drained and rinsed

1 cup new potatoes, parboiled and sliced ⅓-inch thick

2 white bread slices

6 tablespoons butter or margarine, divided

- Preheat oven to 350°.
- Combine ⅔ teaspoon rosemary, sugar, ½ teaspoon salt, and ¼ teaspoon pepper.
- Toss with fruit and vegetables.
- Pour into a 9 x 13-inch pan.
- Cover and bake for 30 minutes.
- Crumble bread slices to make crumbs.
- Toss bread crumbs with 2 tablespoons butter, 1½ teaspoons salt and ¼ teaspoon pepper.
- Dot 4 tablespoons butter over baked casserole and top with bread crumbs.
- Increase oven temperature to 400° and return casserole to oven until lightly browned.

Serves 6 to 8

DESSERTS

Show Thyme

Show Thyme

Show thyme is just about any thyme in Paducah. Throughout the year, there are a variety of plays and concerts to delight, amuse, and entertain a wide range of audiences. For the theatre lover, there are year round musical and drama productions at the Market House Theater and Paducah Community College. In addition to a multitude of live performances, Paducahans can enjoy special screenings of artistic films offered by the Paducah Film Society. The Charity League Follies, reminiscent of the old Vaudeville shows, is a fun and fundraising performance with local talent singing and dancing to benefit area charities. For the finest in music, the Paducah Symphony orchestra and chorus provides a concert series featuring the highly popular annual Christmas performance. During the summer months, musicians and performers draw crowds from all over the region on Saturday nights with eclectic sidewalk entertainment.

Performing arts patrons like to entertain as well as be entertained, and after the final curtain call, enjoy getting together to critique and discuss what they have seen and heard. Sharing honors on the play bill or concert program is cuisine to delight the senses. The grand finale to a delightful afternoon or evening can be a light supper or after-dinner cheese, wine and fruit, sinfully rich desserts such as *Decadent Chocolate Cake* (page 174) and *Strawberry Glazed Cheesecake* (page 177), and a variety of special blend coffees.

A round of applause, please, for a stellar performance and award-winning desserts.

Curtain Call
Dessert and Coffee Party

Coffee Orleans

Tuxedo Cake

Paducah's Best Peanut Butter Pie

Strawberry-Glazed Cheesecake

Ruby Red Shortbread Cookies

Show Thyme:

Lights: There can never be too many candles.
Camera: Take pictures of your table, your decorations and your guests!
Action: Provide activities that will make your guests comfortable and included.

Theatre In the Round—If space allows, use round tables for good conversation.

A Show Stopper—Always be prepared in case something goes wrong. No one expects perfection, but it's nice to have a back-up plan.

Chocolate Mousse Terrine with Raspberry Coulis

Elegant and rich.

2 cups heavy cream, divided

2 (8 ounce) packages semi-sweet
   chocolate squares

½ cup light corn syrup

½ cup butter

¼ cup confectioners' sugar,
   sifted

1 teaspoon vanilla

1 (10 ounce) package frozen
   raspberries, thawed or 1½
   cups fresh raspberries

- Line a 9 x 5-inch loaf pan with plastic wrap, having edges wrap over sides of pan. Set aside.

- In a large, heavy saucepan combine ½ cup heavy cream, chocolate squares, corn syrup and butter. Cook over low heat, stirring constantly until chocolate melts. Remove from heat and allow to cool.

- In another bowl, beat remaining 1½ cups heavy cream, confectioners' sugar and vanilla at high speed until stiff peaks form.

- Fold whipped cream into chocolate mixture.

- Pour into prepared pan; cover and chill for at least 8 hours.

- Process raspberries in a blender until smooth, stopping to scrape down sides.

- Using a fine wire-mesh strainer, pour purée through to separate seeds from liquid; discards seeds. Chill purée.

- To serve, invert mousse onto serving platter and remove plastic wrap. Slice and serve with purée.

Variation: Can use 1½ cups fresh raspberries.

Serves 16

Tuxedo Cake

1 (14 ounce) package angel food cake

6 tablespoons light rum

1 (12 ounce) package semi-sweet chocolate chips

3 eggs

1 tablespoon vanilla extract

¼ teaspoon salt

1½ pints heavy cream, divided

2 tablespoons sugar

3 tablespoons confectioners' sugar

¼ cup toasted, slivered almonds for garnish

Chocolate shavings for garnish

- Slice cake into 2-inch pieces and arrange on a cookie sheet. Sprinkle cake with rum. Set aside.
- Melt chocolate chips in a double boiler, stirring frequently until smooth.
- Add eggs one at a time, stirring well after each addition.
- Add vanilla and salt and cook, stirring for 1 minute. Remove from heat and cool slightly.
- Whip ½ pint of the heavy cream, adding sugar gradually until stiff peaks form. Fold into chocolate mixture.
- In a buttered 9-inch springform pan, alternate cake and chocolate mixture, beginning and ending with the cake (there should be 3 layers of cake and 2 layers of chocolate).
- Cover and refrigerate for at least 6 hours.
- Remove from refrigerator and run a sharp knife around sides of pan to loosen cake. Remove sides of pan.
- Whip remaining heavy cream with confectioners' sugar until stiff peaks form. Generously frost top and sides of cake.
- Garnish as desired or use ¼ cup toasted, slivered almonds or chocolate shavings.
- Store in refrigerator or cover and freeze.

Serves 12 to 16

"Entertaining involves all the senses: sight, sound, smell, taste, and touch."

Chocolate Raspberry Trifle

An elegant finale.

Cake:
2 eggs
½ cup sugar
½ cup self-rising flour
½ teaspoon vanilla

1 cup raspberry jam
¼ cup Crème de Cacao

Custard:
3 tablespoons sugar
1 tablespoon flour
2 eggs
2 cups milk, divided
½ teaspoon vanilla

2 ounces semi-sweet chocolate
½ cup heavy cream
1 tablespoon confectioners'
  sugar
¼ cup slivered almonds for
  garnish
Whipped cream for garnish

- Preheat oven to 350°.
- To prepare cake, beat eggs until frothy. Beat in sugar. Gradually fold in flour. Add vanilla and mix well.
- Pour batter into a greased and floured 8-inch pan. Bake for 25 minutes.
- Remove from oven and cool cake completely. Cut cake into small pieces; line the bottom of a trifle dish with cake pieces.
- Spread a layer of raspberry jam over cake pieces.
- Drizzle Crème de Cacao over jam.
- To prepare custard, combine sugar and flour in a small bowl. Set aside.
- Beat eggs slightly in a medium bowl. Slowly beat sugar and flour mixture into eggs. Set aside.
- In a medium saucepan, scald milk. To scald milk, bring milk to 180° over medium heat. Tiny bubbles should begin to appear around edge of milk just before it reaches 180°.
- Remove milk from heat. Spoon 1 tablespoons of warm milk into egg mixture and mix well. Spoon an additional 2 tablespoons of warm milk into eggs and mix well. This tempers eggs and prevents them from scrambling.
- Slowly pour remaining milk into egg mixture and mix well. Stir in vanilla.
- Pour egg and milk mixture into the top of a double boiler. Cook custard over boiling water, stirring for 10 to 15 minutes until slightly thickened or until custard coats a spoon.
- Remove custard from heat and allow to cool, stirring occasionally to release steam. Custard will continue to thicken as it cools.
- In the trifle dish, cover jam with custard. Cover trifle loosely and chill 20 minutes in refrigerator.

Chocolate Raspberry Trifle

(continued)

- Melt chocolate and drizzle over custard. Chill trifle until ready to serve.
- Before serving trifle, whip heavy cream, gradually adding confectioners' sugar to sweeten. Top trifle with whipped cream and almonds.

Serves 8

Coconut Pound Cake

Exceptionally moist!

3 cups sugar

1½ cups butter, softened

6 eggs

3 cups flour

¼ teaspoon salt

¼ teaspoon baking soda

1 cup sour cream

1 teaspoon coconut extract or
  flavoring

1 (6 ounce) package frozen
  coconut, thawed

Glaze:

¾ cup sugar

½ cup water

1 teaspoon coconut extract or
  flavoring

- Preheat oven to 300°.
- With electric mixer, cream sugar and butter.
- Add eggs one at a time, beating well after each addition.
- Sift together flour, salt and baking soda. Add to sugar mixture, blending thoroughly.
- Stir in sour cream and coconut extract.
- Fold in thawed coconut.
- Pour batter into a well-greased and floured tube pan or Bundt pan.
- Bake for 1½ hours. Remove cake from oven and allow to cool for 20 minutes.
- Meanwhile, prepare glaze by combining all ingredients in a small saucepan. Cook over medium heat. Boil 1 minute. Set aside.
- Invert cake onto a piece of waxed paper, then flip back over onto a serving plate (cake will be upside down).
- Pour glaze over cake.

Serves 12

Kahlúa Cake

1 (18.25 ounce) box devil's food cake mix (without pudding)

1 (3.4 ounce) box instant vanilla pudding

2 eggs

¼ cup vegetable oil

½ cup Kahlúa

1 (16 ounce) container sour cream

1 cup semi-sweet chocolate chips

Confectioners' sugar for sprinkling

- Preheat oven to 350°.
- Combine cake mix, pudding, eggs, oil, Kahlúa and sour cream in a large mixing bowl.
- Stir in chocolate chips.
- Pour batter into a greased Bundt pan.
- Bake for 50 minutes.
- Allow cake to cool; invert cake onto serving plate.
- Dust cake with confectioners' sugar.

Variation: For a special occasion, drizzle cake with dark and white chocolate:

1 (8 ounce) package semi-sweet chocolate squares

1 (8 ounce) package white chocolate squares

- Melt semi-sweet chocolate in a saucepan or double boiler over low heat until smooth.
- Drizzle over cooled cake.
- Melt white chocolate in a saucepan or double boiler over low heat until smooth.
- Drizzle over dark chocolate.

Serves 10 to 12

Amaretto Cake

1 (18.25 ounce) box yellow cake mix

1 (3.4 ounce) box instant vanilla
  pudding

½ cup Amaretto

½ cup water

½ cup vegetable oil

1 teaspoon almond extract

4 eggs

Glaze:

½ cup butter

¼ cup water

½ cup Amaretto

1 cup sugar

- Preheat oven to 325°.
- Combine yellow cake mix, pudding, Amaretto, water, oil, almond extract and eggs in a large mixing bowl. Mix thoroughly.
- Pour batter into a greased Bundt pan.
- Bake for 45 minutes.
- Meanwhile, prepare glaze by melting together butter, water, Amaretto and sugar in a small saucepan. Cook over low heat for 15 to 20 minutes. Set aside and allow to cool slightly.
- Remove cake from oven, allow to cool for 15 minutes and invert onto serving plate.
- Drizzle glaze over cake.
- Note: Delicious served plain or garnished with fruit and whipped cream.

Serves 10 to 12

Plum Cake

A "comfort" food. Serve warm.

2 cups sugar

2 cups self-rising flour

1 teaspoon cloves

1 teaspoon cinnamon

2 (4 ounce) jars plum baby food

¾ cup oil

3 eggs

½ cup coconut

½ cup chopped pecans

1 teaspoon vanilla

Icing:

½ cup butter or margarine

¾ teaspoon baking soda

1 cup buttermilk

1 cup sugar

- Preheat oven to 350°.
- Mix by hand: sugar, flour, cloves and cinnamon.
- Add baby food, oil, eggs, coconut, pecans and vanilla. Blend well.
- Pour batter into greased and floured 9 x 13-inch baking dish.
- Bake for 35 to 40 minutes.
- Meanwhile, prepare icing by combining all ingredients in a small saucepan. Boil 1 minute. Remove from heat and set aside.
- Remove cake from oven and with a fork, punch several holes over surface of cake.
- Pour warm icing over cake, allowing icing to drain down into holes.

Serves 12 to 15

Decadent Chocolate Cake

A thin sheet cake with creamy icing.

2 cups sugar

2 cups flour

½ teaspoon salt

½ teaspoon baking soda

1 cup butter or margarine

4 tablespoons cocoa powder

1 cup water

2 eggs

½ cup sour cream

1 teaspoon vanilla

Icing:

½ cup butter or margarine

4 tablespoons cocoa powder

6 tablespoons milk

1 (16 ounce) box confectioners'
    sugar

½ teaspoon vanilla

One squirt of lemon juice

- Preheat oven to 350°.
- Combine sugar, flour, salt and baking soda in a large bowl. Set aside.
- In a double boiler, melt butter, cocoa powder and water. Stir until smooth.
- Pour chocolate mixture into dry ingredients and stir until well mixed.
- Add eggs, sour cream and vanilla. Mix thoroughly.
- Pour batter into a greased 10 x 15-inch baking pan.
- Bake for 40 minutes.
- Meanwhile, prepare icing by melting butter, cocoa powder and milk in a double boiler. Stir until smooth. Remove from heat.
- Whisk in confectioners' sugar, vanilla and lemon juice. Continue stirring until icing is smooth.
- Pour icing over warm cake. Allow cake to cool until icing is set.

Serves 16

> *"Inform the neighbors of your party plans. Better yet, invite them over!"*

Harvest Pumpkin Cake

2 cups sugar

4 eggs, beaten

1 cup vegetable oil

2 cups flour

2 teaspoons baking soda

2 teaspoons cinnamon

½ teaspoon salt

2 cups pumpkin

Icing:

¼ cup butter, softened

1 (3 ounce) package cream
    cheese, softened

1 cup confectioners' sugar

½ cup chopped pecans or walnuts

½ teaspoon vanilla

- Preheat oven to 350°.
- Blend together sugar and eggs in a large bowl.
- Add vegetable oil and mix well. Set aside.
- In a separate bowl, sift together flour, baking soda, cinnamon and salt.
- Add dry ingredients to sugar mixture.
- Stir in pumpkin, mixing well.
- Pour batter into a greased Bundt pan. Bake for 1 hour or until knife inserted in center comes out clean.
- Allow cake to cool and invert onto serving plate.
- For icing, beat butter with cream cheese until smooth.
- Slowly add confectioners' sugar until all is incorporated.
- Stir in nuts and vanilla.
- Ice top of cake only.

Serves 10 to 12

"The Best" Cheesecake

Crust:

1½ cups graham cracker crumbs

¼ cup sugar

½ cup butter, melted

Filling:

4 (8 ounce) packages cream
    cheese, softened

1 cup sugar

1 teaspoon vanilla

6 eggs

Topping:

2 cups sour cream

1½ cups sugar

1 teaspoon vanilla

Cinnamon for sprinkling

- Preheat oven to 350°.
- Prepare crust by mixing together all ingredients. Press into a buttered 9-inch springform pan.
- Bake crust for 5 minutes.
- For filling, mix cream cheese, sugar and vanilla. Add eggs one at a time, beating well after each addition.
- Pour filling into crust and bake for 50 to 55 minutes until golden brown. Top should start to crack.
- Meanwhile, prepare topping: mix sour cream, sugar and vanilla.
- Remove cake from oven, top with sour cream mixture and sprinkle lightly with cinnamon. Return cake to oven for 10 minutes.
- Allow cake to cool to room temperature, cover and refrigerate overnight.

Serves 16

Heavenly Strawberry Cake

1 (18.25 ounce) box white cake
  mix

½ cup vegetable oil

½ cup water

1 (3 ounce) box strawberry
  gelatin

3 eggs

1 (10 ounce) package frozen
  strawberries, thawed and
  drained (reserve juice for
  icing)

Icing:

½ cup butter, softened

1 (16 ounce) box confectioners'
  sugar

¼ cup reserved strawberry juice

- Preheat oven to 350°.
- Combine cake mix, oil, water and gelatin in a large mixing bowl.
- Add eggs one at a time to mix, blending thoroughly after each addition.
- Gently fold in strawberries.
- Pour batter into greased and floured 9 x 13-inch baking pan.
- Bake for 35 to 40 minutes.
- For icing, mix together all ingredients until smooth and spread over cooled cake.

*Variation: For a round layer cake, substitute two
8- or 9-inch round cake pans and decrease baking
time to 25 to 30 minutes.*

Serves 12

"Pleasantest of all ties is the tie of host and guest."

Aeschylus

Strawberry-Glazed Cheesecake

Crust:

¾ cup coarsely ground walnuts

¾ cup finely crushed graham crackers

3 tablespoons unsalted butter, melted

Filling:

4 (8 ounce) packages cream cheese, softened

4 eggs

1¼ cups sugar

1 tablespoon fresh lemon juice

2 teaspoons vanilla

Topping:

2 cups sour cream

¼ cup sugar

1 teaspoon vanilla

Strawberry Glaze:

1 quart medium to large strawberries

1 (12 ounce) jar red raspberry jelly (do not substitute jam or preserves)

1 tablespoon cornstarch

¼ cup Cointreau or Triple Sec

¼ cup water

- Position rack in center of oven and preheat oven to 350°.

- To prepare crust, combine walnuts, graham cracker crumbs and butter. Press firmly onto bottom of a lightly buttered 9- or 10-inch springform pan. Set aside.

- For filling, beat cream cheese in a large bowl until smooth.

- Add eggs, sugar, lemon juice and vanilla. Beat thoroughly.

- Spoon mixture over crust.

- Bake a 9-inch cake for 50 to 55 minutes. Bake a 10-inch cake for 40 to 45 minutes. Cake may rise slightly and crack in several places; it will settle and most cracks will be minimal.

- Meanwhile, prepare topping. Combine sour cream, sugar and vanilla. Mix well. Refrigerate.

- Remove cake from oven. Allow to stand at room temperature for 15 minutes. Retain oven temperature at 350°.

- Spoon topping over cake, starting at center and extending to within ½ inch of edge. Return to oven and bake 5 minutes.

- Allow cake to cool. Refrigerate covered cake overnight.

- To prepare glaze, wash and cap strawberries. Let dry completely on paper towels.

- In a small saucepan, combine 1 tablespoon jelly with cornstarch, mixing well. Add remaining jelly, Cointreau and water. Cook over medium heat, stirring frequently until thickened and clear; about 5 to 7 minutes. Cool to lukewarm, stirring occasionally.

- Using a knife, loosen cake from pan and remove sides. Arrange berries with pointed ends up over top of cake. Spoon glaze over berries, allowing some to drip down sides.

- Refrigerate until glaze is set.

Serves 12

German Gingerbread

1 (16 ounce) box brown sugar
2 cups flour
¾ cup butter
1 teaspoon baking soda
2 teaspoons cinnamon
1 teaspoon nutmeg
1 teaspoon ginger
½ teaspoon cloves
2 eggs
1 cup buttermilk
Whipped cream, for garnish

- Preheat oven to 325°.
- Combine brown sugar, flour and butter together in a medium mixing bowl until crumbly. Reserve 1 cup mixture for cake topping.
- Add baking soda, cinnamon, nutmeg, ginger and cloves to remaining flour mixture. Blend well.
- Add eggs and buttermilk; combine.
- Pour batter into a greased 9 x 13-inch baking pan.
- Sprinkle batter evenly with reserved flour mixture.
- Bake for 30 to 40 minutes.
- Serve warm with whipped cream.

Serves 12 to 16

Southern Pecan Pie

A must for Thanksgiving.

1 ready-to-bake pie crust
4 large eggs
¾ cup sugar
½ teaspoon salt
¼ teaspoon cinnamon
¼ teaspoon nutmeg
1½ cups dark corn syrup
    (canned if available)
⅓ cup butter, melted
1 teaspoon pure vanilla
1½ cups chopped pecans

- Grease pie plate and line with pie shell. Place in refrigerator to chill.
- Preheat oven to 350°.
- Meanwhile, beat together eggs, sugar and salt in a large mixing bowl.
- Add cinnamon, nutmeg, corn syrup, butter and vanilla. Combine thoroughly.
- Remove chilled pie shell from refrigerator and spread pecans evenly over bottom of the crust.
- Pour filling over pecans.
- Bake for 1 hour or until firm.
- Note: Serve warm with vanilla ice cream.

Serves 8

Southern Delight Pie

Very rich!

1 cup sugar
½ cup flour
2 eggs
½ cup butter, melted
1 teaspoon vanilla
1 cup butterscotch chips
1 cup chopped pecans
½ cup flaked coconut
1 unbaked deep-dish pie shell
Whipped cream for garnish

- Preheat oven to 350°.
- Lightly combine sugar, flour and eggs in a large mixing bowl.
- Add butter and vanilla. Mix well.
- Stir in butterscotch chips, pecans and coconut.
- Pour mixture into unbaked pie shell.
- Bake for 45 to 50 minutes.
- Note: Garnish with whipped cream.

Serves 6 to 8

Red's Peach Pie

Great in the summer when local peaches are in season.

Crust:
1 cup flour
¼ cup confectioners' sugar
½ cup butter or margarine

Filling:
1 (8 ounce) package cream cheese, softened
1 cup confectioners' sugar
1 (8 ounce) container non-dairy whipped topping
3 cups sliced fresh peaches
Powdered fruit preservative

Glaze:
1 cup sugar
4 tablespoons cornstarch
3 tablespoons peach gelatin
1 (10 ounce) bottle lemon-lime soda

- If making own crust, mix ingredients together with a fork and press into two 8-inch pie pans.
- For filling, beat cream cheese, confectioners' sugar and whipped topping together. Spread over pie crusts.
- Layer peaches (1½ cups per pie) over cream cheese mixture and sprinkle with fruit preservative. Set aside.
- To make glaze, combine sugar, cornstarch, peach gelatin and lemon-lime soda in a small saucepan. Bring to a boil. Cook until thick and clear.
- Spread glaze over peaches.
- Chill pies in refrigerator before serving.

Variation: Can use 2 (8-inch) prepared butter crust pie shells.

Yields 2 (8-inch) pies, serving 16 total

"Run for the Roses" Derby Pie

Be sure to serve this on the first Saturday in May.

1 ready-to-bake pie crust
2 eggs
½ cup butter, melted
⅓ cup flour
1 cup sugar
1 tablespoon bourbon
  (or 1 teaspoon vanilla)
Dash of salt
1 cup semi-sweet chocolate chips
1 cup chopped pecans
Whipped cream or vanilla ice
  cream for garnish

- Preheat oven to 325°.
- Press pie crust into the bottom of a greased and floured 9-inch glass pie plate.
- Beat eggs until frothy.
- Add butter, flour, sugar, bourbon and salt to eggs.
- Mix until well blended. Stir in chocolate chips and pecans.
- Pour mixture into pie crust and bake for 50 to 60 minutes or until pie is golden and firm.
- Serve topped with whipped cream and/or ice cream.

Serves 8

Paducah's Best Peanut Butter Pie

Make this pie in less than 10 minutes!

1 (8 ounce) package cream
  cheese, softened
1 cup confectioners' sugar
1 cup creamy peanut butter
½ cup milk
1 (8 ounce) container non-dairy
  whipped topping
1 chocolate sandwich cookie-
  flavored pie crust
Whipped cream for garnish
Peanut butter cup miniatures,
  coarsely chopped for garnish

- Beat cream cheese, confectioners' sugar, peanut butter and milk together until smooth.
- Gently fold in whipped topping until well blended.
- Pour mixture into pie crust. Smooth mixture evenly to edges of crust.
- Cover pie and refrigerate.
- One hour prior to serving, place pie in freezer to chill completely.
- Slice and serve, garnishing as desired.
- Note: For a festive presentation, garnish each slice with whipped cream and coarsely chopped peanut butter cup miniatures.

Serves 6 to 8

Grasshopper Pie

16 chocolate sandwich cookies, finely crushed

4 tablespoons butter, melted

24 large marshmallows

⅔ cup milk

½ pint heavy cream, whipped

2 ounces Crème De Menthe

2 ounces Crème De Cacao

Garnish:
 Additional whipped cream

- To prepare crust, combine crushed cookies and butter. Press into bottom and sides of a 9-inch pie plate. Set aside.
- In a large saucepan, melt marshmallows in milk. Remove from heat; cool.
- Fold in whipped heavy cream and liqueurs. Blend well.
- Pour mixture into crust.
- Freeze pie for at least 2 hours before serving.
- Serve topped with additional whipped cream.
- Note: This pie freezes well.

Serves 8

Blackberry and Apple Pie

2½ pounds apples, peeled, cored and sliced

2 cups fresh or frozen blackberries

1 cup sugar

1½ teaspoons cinnamon

½ teaspoon nutmeg

2 tablespoons flour

1 (15 ounce) box refrigerated pie crusts (both crusts in box will be used)

1 tablespoon butter, softened

1 egg yolk

1 tablespoon milk

- Preheat oven to 375°.
- Mix apples and blackberries in a large bowl. Set aside.
- Blend sugar, cinnamon, nutmeg and flour in a small bowl. Gently mix into fruit. Set aside.
- Press one pie crust into a lightly greased 9-inch pie plate. Dot with softened butter.
- Spoon fruit mixture into crust.
- Top with remaining pie crust, crimping edges of both crusts together. Fruit should be sealed inside shell.
- Whisk the egg yolk with milk; brush mixture over top of pie.
- Pierce top crust several times with a knife to allow steam to escape.
- Bake for 1 hour and 15 minutes until apples are tender when poked with a thin knife.
- Note: If crust seems to be browning too quickly, reduce heat to 325°.

Variation: Substitute fresh peaches for the apples when the local peach crop arrives.

Serves 8

Key Lime Pie

Refreshing on a hot summer day!

2 (14 ounce) cans sweetened
    condensed milk
4 egg yolks, beaten
¾ cup lime juice
1 tablespoon grated lime zest
1 (9-inch) graham cracker crust
2 cups heavy cream
2 tablespoons confectioners'
    sugar, sifted
½ teaspoon vanilla
1 lime slice for garnish

- Preheat oven to 300°.
- Combine condensed milk, egg yolks, lime juice and zest.
- Pour filling into pie crust and bake for 10 to 15 minutes.
- Allow pie to cool.
- Refrigerate pie for 1 hour.
- Meanwhile, to prepare whipped cream, beat heavy cream at high speed until soft peaks form.
- Fold in confectioners' sugar and vanilla.
- Top pie with whipped cream.
- Garnish with a lime slice in the center of pie.

Serves 8

Old-Fashioned Strawberry Pie

1 baked pie crust
1-1½ quarts fresh strawberries
1 cup sugar
4 tablespoons cornstarch

- Wash, dry and cap strawberries.
- Place half of strawberries into pie crust.
- Slightly mash remaining strawberries in a saucepan.
- Bring to a boil. Mix in sugar and cornstarch. Cook slowly for 10 minutes, stirring often.
- Let cool. Pour berries into pie crust.
- Top with whipped cream and serve.
- Note: In choosing strawberries, remember the smaller berries are usually sweeter.

Serves 8 to 10

Fabulous Fudge Pie

If you love chocolate, you will love this pie!

½ cup butter or margarine,
   melted
1⅓ cups sugar
2 heaping tablespoons cocoa
   powder
3 eggs
Dash of salt
1 (9-inch) unbaked pie shell
Whipped cream for garnish

- Preheat oven to 350°.
- Combine butter, sugar, cocoa powder, eggs and salt in a large mixing bowl. Beat thoroughly with mixer or wire whisk.
- Pour mixture into pie shell.
- Bake for 30 to 35 minutes or until center of pie is firm.
- Allow to cool slightly before serving.
- Note: This pie is good topped with a dollop of whipped cream.

Serves 8

"*Every guest is important, even the little ones. Don't hesitate to invite youngsters to the 'big' table. They'll feel important and included.*"

Blackberry Cobbler

Cream cheese crust makes this cobbler special.

Pastry:
1 cup unsalted butter, softened

*1 (8 ounce) package cream
    cheese, softened*

1 teaspoon vanilla

2 cups flour

Cobbler:
*6 cups fresh blackberries, rinsed
    and dried*

1½ cups sugar

¼ cup cornstarch

1 teaspoon lemon juice

- To prepare pastry, cream butter, cream cheese and vanilla in a mixing bowl.
- Gradually sift flour into bowl, mixing with a fork until a ball of dough forms. Add more flour to dough if sticky.
- Divide dough in half. Wrap in plastic wrap and refrigerate for 45 minutes or overnight.
- Preheat oven to 400°.
- Roll both pastries to ⅛-inch thickness using short, even strokes and dusting with flour as needed.
- Lightly grease a 10-inch baking dish or tartlet pan. Drape one crust over sides of pan, lining the bottom. Press firmly into pan. Prick bottom of crust with fork and bake for 15 to 20 minutes until slightly golden.
- Remove from oven and set aside.
- To prepare filling, combine berries, sugar, cornstarch and lemon juice in a large bowl.
- Pour into crust.
- Top berries with remaining dough, either in a lattice design or in tartlet design.
- Bake 35 to 40 minutes or until golden brown.

Serves 6

"Sophisticated people like informal parties."

Raspberry Sweet Tart

1 (16 ounce) package phyllo
  dough

1 (8 ounce) package cream
  cheese, softened

2 cups confectioners' sugar

1 (8 ounce) container non-dairy
  whipped topping

½ teaspoon almond extract

6 tablespoons butter, melted

Sugar for sprinkling on dough

6 tablespoons honey, warmed

Cinnamon for sprinkling on
  dough

1 egg white, beaten

Raspberry Sauce:

1 (10 ounce) package frozen
  raspberries thawed and
  strained to remove seeds

½ teaspoon orange extract

1½ cups sugar

Dash of cinnamon

- Preheat oven to 350°.
- Unfold phyllo, making a large rectangle of dough layers. Set aside.
- Blend cream cheese, confectioners' sugar, whipped topping and almond extract. Fluff with mixer. Set filling aside.
- Alternating layers of pastry, prepare dough as follows: spread first layer with a thin coat of melted butter topped with a sprinkling of sugar; second layer should be brushed with warm honey topped with a sprinkling of cinnamon. Continue brushing alternate layers with either butter or honey as directed until entire pastry is sweetened.
- Spread cream cheese filling on top of sweetened pastry. Beginning with a long end of the dough rectangle, roll pastry jelly roll style until rounded.
- Brush top of jelly roll tart with beaten egg white.
- Seal ends of roll by pinching sides together.
- Lay roll on a jelly-roll pan (or cookie sheet with a lip) that has been buttered and sprinkled with sugar.
- Bake for 30 minutes or until lightly browned.
- Allow pastry to cool before slicing.
- To prepare raspberry sauce, add raspberries, sugar, orange extract, and cinnamon to a small saucepan. Simmer on low heat, stirring occasionally for 15 minutes.
- Serve individual tart slices garnished with warm sauce, whipped cream and slivered almonds.

Serves 8

Tilghman Choir Brownies

A local high school choir sells these treats each year for its fundraiser. The brownies always sell quickly!

2 (19.8 ounce) boxes brownie
    mix
1 cup miniature marshmallows
¾ cup semi-sweet chocolate chips

Icing:
½ cup butter or margarine
4 tablespoons cocoa powder
6 tablespoons milk
1 (16 ounce) box confectioners'
    sugar, sifted
1 teaspoon vanilla

- Empty two boxes brownie mix into a large mixing bowl and prepare according to package instructions, doubling ingredients since two brownie packages are being used.
- Stir in marshmallows and chocolate chips.
- Pour batter into greased 9 x 13-inch baking dish.
- Bake according to package instructions for a 9 x 13-inch pan plus an additional 20 minutes.
- Meanwhile, prepare icing. Combine butter, cocoa powder and milk in saucepan and bring to a slow boil. Boil 2 minutes. Remove from heat and add confectioners' sugar and vanilla, whisking to combine.
- As soon as brownies come out of oven, pour icing over top and let cool for several hours until icing is set.

Yields 24 brownies

Mocha Brownies with Coffee Frosting

4 eggs

2 cups sugar

1 cup vegetable oil

10 tablespoons cocoa powder

2 teaspoons vanilla

1½ cups flour

2 teaspoons salt

1 cup chopped walnuts

Frosting:

2 heaping tablespoons cocoa
    powder

3 tablespoons butter

1 (16 ounce) box confectioners'
    sugar

4 tablespoons hot brewed coffee

Additional milk to thin frosting,
    if necessary

- Preheat oven to 350°.
- Whisk eggs together until frothy.
- Add sugar, oil, cocoa powder and vanilla to eggs, mixing well.
- In a separate bowl, sift together flour and salt. Add to egg mixture and mix well.
- Add walnuts, if desired.
- Pour batter into a greased 9 x 13-inch baking dish. Bake for 30 to 35 minutes.
- While brownies are baking, prepare frosting by mixing cocoa powder, butter and 1 cup confectioners' sugar together in a medium saucepan. Cook over low heat, stirring constantly.
- When frosting is warm, add coffee and mix.
- Continue to add remaining confectioners' sugar, stirring constantly until thick.
- If necessary, milk may be added to frosting to thin consistency.
- Frost brownies while they are still slightly warm.

Yields 24 brownies

"Every house where love abides and friendship is great is surely home, and home sweet home; for there the heart can rest."

Henry Van Dyke

Applesauce Oaties

A wonderful chewy cookie!

1¾ cups quick cook oats, uncooked

1½ cups flour

1 teaspoon salt

1 teaspoon baking powder

1 teaspoon cinnamon

½ teaspoon nutmeg

½ teaspoon baking soda

½ cup butter, softened

1 cup firmly packed brown sugar

½ cup sugar

1 egg

¾ cup applesauce

1 (6 ounce) package semi-sweet chocolate morsels

1 cup raisins

1 cup chopped nuts

- Preheat oven to 375°.
- Combine oats, flour, salt, baking powder, cinnamon, nutmeg and baking soda. Set aside.
- Cream butter, brown sugar and sugar. Beat until creamy.
- Beat in egg.
- Gradually mix in flour mixture, alternating with applesauce.
- Stir in chocolate morsels, raisins and nuts.
- Drop by tablespoons on a lightly greased cookie sheet.
- Bake for 12 to 14 minutes.

Yields 5 dozen cookies

Awesome Chocolate Chip Cookies

1 cup butter, softened
1 cup sugar
1 cup firmly packed dark brown
    sugar
2 large eggs
1 teaspoon baking soda
¾ teaspoon salt
2 cups flour
2 tablespoons vanilla
1 (12 ounce) bag chocolate chips

- Preheat oven to 350°.
- Cream butter, sugar and brown sugar until smooth.
- Beat in eggs.
- In a separate bowl, combine baking soda, salt and flour. Add to butter mixture and stir well.
- Blend in vanilla.
- Stir in chocolate chips.
- Round dough into balls and place on an ungreased cookie sheet.
- Bake for 8 to 10 minutes or until golden brown.
- Note: Allow ample room for the dough to spread on your cookie sheet — these cookies are large, thin and crispy.

Yields approximately 50 cookies

Chocolate Sugar Cookies

3 (1 ounce) squares unsweetened
    chocolate
1 cup butter
1 cup sugar
1 egg
1 teaspoon vanilla
2 cups flour
1 teaspoon baking soda
¼ teaspoon salt
½-1 cup sugar for coating
    cookies

- Preheat oven to 375°.
- Combine chocolate squares and butter in a medium microwave-safe bowl. Microwave 2 minutes. Remove and stir until chocolate is melted completely.
- In a large mixing bowl, combine sugar and chocolate mixture. Stir well.
- Blend in egg and vanilla.
- Add flour, baking soda and salt. Mix dough thoroughly.
- Cover and refrigerate 30 minutes.
- Shape dough into balls and roll in additional sugar to coat.
- Place 2 inches apart on an ungreased cookie sheet and bake for 8 to 10 minutes.

Yields 3 dozen cookies

Ruby Red Shortbread Cookies

A sweet ending to a bridal luncheon or baby shower.

1 cup butter, softened

⅔ cup sugar

1 teaspoon vanilla extract

½ teaspoon almond extract

2 cups flour

1 (18 ounce) jar raspberry
    preserves, for topping

Glaze:

1 cup confectioners' sugar

1½ teaspoons vanilla extract

3 teaspoons water

- Cream butter, sugar and extracts together until smooth.
- Slowly add flour, mixing dough well.
- Cover dough and allow to chill in refrigerator for 2 hours.
- Preheat oven to 350°.
- Roll dough into small balls, spacing 2 inches apart on an ungreased cookie sheet.
- Using index finger, press a small indention into center of each cookie. Fill with a small amount of preserves.
- Bake cookies for 15 to 18 minutes. Edges will crack and be lightly browned.
- Remove cookies from oven and allow to stand on cookie sheet for 2 minutes.
- Remove cookies from cookie sheet and cool completely.
- For glaze, mix all ingredients in a small bowl. Drizzle glaze over cookies.

Variation: For a delicious twist, add ground pecans or ground almonds to the dough. Or substitute strawberry preserves for a different berry taste.

Yields approximately 30 cookies

Simple Sand Tarts

6 tablespoons confectioners'
    sugar

1 cup butter, softened

2 cups flour

1 teaspoon vanilla

1½ cups crushed pecans

Additional confectioners' sugar
    for coating

- Preheat oven to 350°.
- Cream sugar and butter in large mixing bowl.
- Add flour and vanilla, mixing well.
- Stir in pecans.
- Shape dough into 1-inch balls and bake for 15 minutes on an ungreased cookie sheet.
- When cookies are cool, roll in additional confectioners' sugar to coat.

Yields 2 to 3 dozen cookies

Almond Crunch Cookies

1 cup sugar
1 cup confectioners' sugar, sifted
1 cup butter, softened
1 cup vegetable oil
2 eggs
2 teaspoons almond extract
4½ cups flour
1 teaspoon baking soda
1 teaspoon salt
1 teaspoon cream of tartar
2 cups chopped almonds
1 (6 ounce) bag almond brickle chips

- Cream together sugar, confectioners' sugar, butter and oil in a large mixing bowl.
- Beat in eggs, almond extract, flour, baking soda, salt and cream of tartar. Mix thoroughly.
- Stir in almonds and brickle chips.
- Cover dough and chill overnight in refrigerator.
- Preheat oven to 350°.
- Roll dough into 1½-inch balls, spacing them 3 inches apart on ungreased cookie sheet.
- Using the tines of a fork, press tops of cookies twice to make a crisscross pattern.
- Bake for 14 to 15 minutes.
- Note: These cookies also freeze well.

Yields approximately 50 cookies

Amaretto Cheesecake Bars

3 (8 ounce) packages cream cheese, softened
¾ cup sugar
4 tablespoons Amaretto
3 eggs
1½ cups graham cracker crumbs
½ cup sliced almonds
⅓ cup butter, melted
3 tablespoons sugar

- Preheat oven to 350°.
- Mix cream cheese, sugar and Amaretto until well blended.
- Add eggs; set aside.
- Mix graham cracker crumbs, almonds, melted butter and sugar. Press into a 13 x 9-inch pan.
- Pour batter over crust.
- Bake for 30 minutes. Cool.
- Refrigerate a minimum of 3 hours. Cut into bars.

Yields 24 bars

Favorite Holiday Fudge

2 cups sugar

1 cup heavy cream

¼ teaspoon salt

2 (1 ounce) squares unsweetened
chocolate

1 teaspoon vanilla

1 tablespoon butter

1 cup chopped pecans

- Mix sugar, cream and salt in large, heavy saucepan.
  Bring to a boil over medium heat.

- Add chocolate; reduce heat to medium-low. Stir sparingly, only enough to keep chocolate from sticking.

- Cook to a soft ball stage (240°F on a candy
  thermometer).

- Remove from heat. Stir in vanilla and butter.

- Tilt pan to side and beat with a large wooden spoon. At
  first, chocolate will be thin and shiny. It should begin to
  thicken and lose its luster.

- Add pecans just as chocolate starts to thicken and look
  dull.

- Pour fudge into a buttered 9 x 9-inch dish.

- Refrigerate 2 hours before cutting into squares.

Yields 2 dozen pieces

Incredible Edibles

Children love these snacks! Serve these treats at your child's next classroom party.

2 cups graham cracker crumbs

2 cups confectioners' sugar

1 (12 ounce) jar creamy peanut
butter

¾ cup butter or margarine,
melted

1 (12 ounce) package semi-sweet
chocolate chips

- In a large bowl, mix graham cracker crumbs,
  confectioners' sugar, peanut butter and butter.

- Spread batter evenly in an ungreased 9 x 13-inch baking
  pan. Set aside.

- Melt chocolate chips in a double boiler or microwave
  until smooth.

- Spread melted chocolate over peanut butter mixture.

- Chill in refrigerator at least one hour before serving.

- Before cutting, allow to stand at room temperature for a
  few minutes to prevent chocolate from cracking.

Serves 15

Blueberry Citrus Bars

1 cup butter, softened

¾ cup confectioners' sugar, sifted

2¼ cups flour, divided

4 eggs

1½ cups sugar

⅓ cup fresh lemon juice

2 tablespoons finely shredded orange peel

1 teaspoon baking powder

1½ cups fresh blueberries

Powdered sugar for garnish

- Preheat oven to 350°.

- To make crust, beat butter for 30 seconds. Mix in confectioners' sugar. Slowly add 2 cups flour.

- Press crust firmly into a greased 9 x 13-inch pan.

- Bake for 20 minutes or until golden brown.

- To make filling, combine eggs, sugar, lemon juice, orange peel, ¼ cup flour and baking powder in a large mixing bowl. Beat for 2 minutes.

- Sprinkle berries over crust. Pour filling over berries, arranging berries evenly.

- Return pan to oven and bake for an additional 30 to 35 minutes of until filling is set.

- Cool before cutting. Sprinkle with powdered sugar before serving.

- Note: These can be stored in a freezer container for up to 3 months.

Yields 30 bars

"For my celebrations, I usually plan a menu that includes items which can be prepared ahead and then frozen. The money I save on preparing my own food, I spend on hiring a little extra help in the kitchen!"

Miniature Cherry Bon-bon Cheesecakes

Wonderful little edibles!

1 cup crushed chocolate
    sandwich cookies

3 (8 ounce) packages cream
    cheese

1 cup sugar

3 eggs

1 teaspoon vanilla

Topping:

1 (6 ounce) bag semi-sweet
    chocolate chips (or chocolate)

1 (21 ounce) can cherry pie
    filling

- Preheat oven to 350°.
- Place paper candy cups into miniature cupcake pans.
- Line the bottom of each cup with ½ heaping teaspoon of cookie crumbs; pat down.
- Beat cream cheese, sugar and eggs. Add vanilla.
- Fill a pastry tube with cream cheese mixture and pipe over cookie crumbs, almost until the top.
- Bake for 10 minutes or until center is firm.
- Place cupcake pan in refrigerator until cold; remove cakes from pan.
- Melt chocolate chips in a double boiler. Place a small dollop of chocolate on each cheesecake.
- Top each with cherry pie filling before the chocolate hardens.
- Keep refrigerated.

Yields 5½ dozen

Lemon Tartlets

These make a delightful pick up dessert—wonderful for a bridal shower buffet.

½ cup butter, cut in pieces

½ cup sugar

2 tablespoons grated lemon peel

⅓ cup fresh lemon juice

2 eggs, slightly beaten

24 mini phyllo dough shells

Whipped cream for garnish

- Combine butter, sugar, lemon peel, lemon juice and eggs in a saucepan.
- Cook mixture over moderately low heat for 20 to 25 minutes, stirring constantly until curd is thick.
- Transfer curd to a bowl; cool. Cover with wax paper and chill for 1 hour.
- Bake mini phyllo dough shells according to package directions; cool.
- Spoon curd into dough shells.
- Garnish with whipped cream.

Yields 24 tartlets

Top Hat Strawberries

Minimal effort for a beautiful show!

24 large fresh strawberries
1 (8 ounce) package white
  chocolate squares
1 (8 ounce) package semi-sweet
  chocolate squares

- Wash strawberries. Dry berries completely, dabbing gently with paper towels and allowing to air dry on a layer of paper towels.
- Melt white chocolate in a saucepan or double boiler over low heat, stirring until smooth.
- With a cocktail fork, dip each strawberry in the white chocolate ¾ of the way up to the stem. Place berries on waxed paper and cool completely.
- Melt semi-sweet chocolate in another saucepan or double boiler over low heat, stirring until smooth.
- Dip each cooled berry ½ of the way over the white chocolate.
- Place berries on waxed paper and cool completely.
- Arrange on serving platter and cover.
- Refrigerate for up to 2 days.

Yields 24 dipped strawberries

Red Wine Oranges

A light and elegant dessert.

½ cup sugar
1 cup water
1 cup dry red wine
2 whole cloves
2 slices lemon
2 sticks cinnamon
6 to 8 oranges, peeled and
  sectioned

- In a medium saucepan, dissolve sugar in water over medium heat.
- Add wine, cloves, lemon slices and cinnamon sticks.
- Slowly bring mixture to a boil. Boil until slightly syrupy, approximately 20 minutes.
- Strain into a serving bowl; cool 20 minutes.
- Add orange sections and refrigerate for 2 hours or until very cold.

Serves 4

Poached Pears with Cranberries

Very flavorful!

4 ripe pears, stems attached
2 cups cranberry juice
½ cup orange juice
½ cup sugar
1 stick cinnamon
3 whole cloves
½ cup fresh cranberries

- Peel pears with a potato peeler, being careful not to cut stems.
- Remove cores from pears using a paring knife.
- Trim bases with a knife so pears will stand upright. Set pears aside.
- Mix cranberry juice, orange juice and sugar in a large saucepan. Heat to dissolve the sugar.
- Add cinnamon stick and cloves. Boil mixture for 5 minutes.
- Place pears upright in the saucepan; cover pan and simmer for 40 minutes.
- Remove saucepan from heat. Cool completely.
- Chill mixture for at least 2 hours or overnight, turning pears occasionally.
- Remove pears from saucepan. Bring syrup to a boil for 10 minutes until thickened.
- Add cranberries and simmer for an additional 5 minutes. Remove saucepan from heat. Cool.
- Place pears on a serving dish and top with sauce.

Serves 4

"White Christmas-like lights can be draped around your large indoor plants, curtain rods, and buffet tables to create a truly festive and magical atmosphere."

ENTERTAINING GUIDE

Perfect Thyming

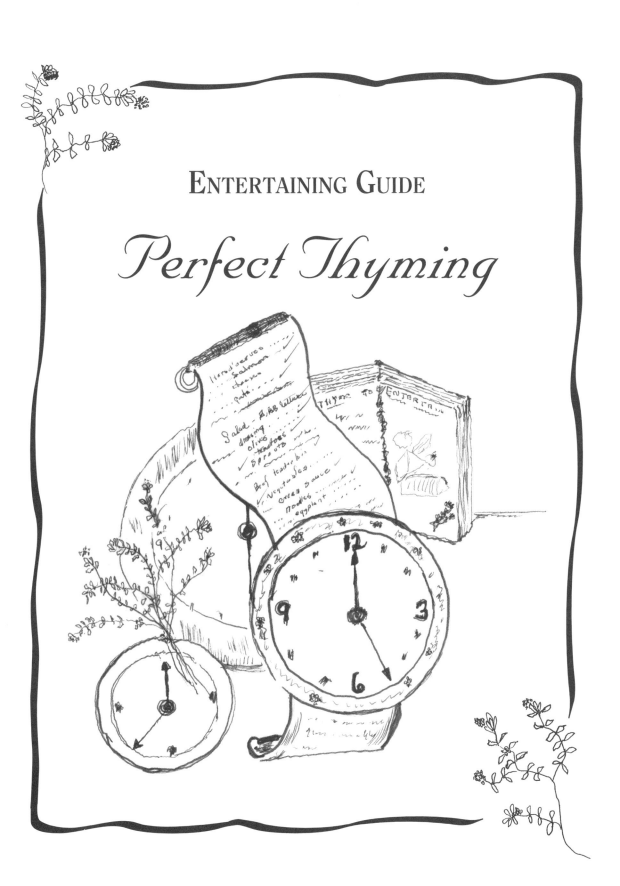

Thymes Remembered

"My mother loved to feed people. If a holiday party were coming up, preparations would start weeks in advance. Every meal would be carefully planned with an abundance of lists and ideas from the appetizer to the after dinner cordials or coffee. After I got married and started entertaining in my own home, I tried to remember just what made everything so special. Of course the food was wonderful but it was more than that. I came up with a list of things that were always a part of her gatherings whether it was just family or two hundred friends.

1. Genuine affection for each and every guest.
2. Great food
3. Fresh flowers
4. Candles
5. Cloth napkins
6. Place cards (often done in crayon by me, the youngest)
7. My dad (Surely everyone knows someone who can light up a room just by being there!)
8. Ability to laugh when something gets burned, forgotten, spilled, broken, etc.
9. The extra effort of using the 'good' china, crystal and silver
10. Thick, soft as cloth, embossed paper guest towels in each bathroom
11. Wonderful music playing in the background (This was my father's responsibility as is now my husband's.)
12. A table large enough for all of us to sit around (even if your sleeve did occasionally brush through your neighbor's butter)
13. The roast or turkey was always carved at the table to allow each person the opportunity to 'ooh' and 'aah.'
14. Special attention and dedication to everyone's favorite dishes.

NOTE: These last few are really more about family gatherings, which my mother believed was the most important entertaining of all.

I admit I can't always find the time to ensure every one of these criteria is met, but I do try to do at least a few of them to make my family and friends feel special. Along the way, I seem to be developing my own unique traditions.

Thanks Mom, I couldn't have done it without you."

Great Thyming Ideas

Whether entertaining in your home or offering a simple gesture of hospitality, timing is everything! A tasty casserole, a fresh green salad, and hot homemade rolls can be a welcomed sight for new parents just home from the hospital with their infant. A well-planned menu featuring a few low fat dishes comes as a relief to your dinner guests who want to indulge and enjoy your meal but don't want to stray too far from their diet. Whatever you are preparing, there is a time and place for everything. We have included a selection of recipes to help you plan your next meal with timing in mind.

Just in the Nick of Thyme—

When you're in a hurry, try these tasty thyme-savers!

Caramel Brie Cheese
Spicy Southwest Penne
Shells with Goat Cheese and Fresh Tomatoes
Honey Glazed Pork Chops
Fresh Green Beans with Feta

Thyme-less Recipes—

Less is more with these wonderful low-fat recipes.

Gazpacho with Gusto
Turkey Scaloppini with Leeks,
　　Currants, and Marsala
Chicken Piccata
Grilled Chicken and Shrimp
Salmon on the Grill
Lemon Vinaigrette Asparagus
Poached Pears with Cranberries
Red Wine Oranges

In Due Thyme—

Take these easy to prepare dishes and desserts to an expecting mother or new mom!

Scrumptious Coffeecake
Chicken Madrid
Chicken and Spinach Puff Bravo
Applesauce Oaties
Almond Crunch Cookies

Thyme out—

Have food will travel! The following are great crowd pleasers for your next potluck.

The Best Apple Dip
"Lettuce Entertain You" Salad
Tri-Color Rotini Salad
Wild Rice and Chicken Salad
Mediterranean Pasta Bake
Summertime Tomatoes

Thyme on your hands?

Prepare these dishes, freeze and pull out when you need them.

Party Cheese Straws
Feta Triangles
Miniature Sausage Quiches
Herbed Chicken Divan
Blueberry Citrus Bars

Party Planning Thymeline

Follow this blueprint for gracious entertaining with ease in your own personal style. Great hospitality is in the details!

One Month Before the Party

- Make a plan. Write down all of your ideas. Select a location.

- Decide upon a theme. Determine your party budget.

- Make lists: guests, party supplies, etc.

- Draw up final guest list. If hosting a large party, go through address book to be sure you have not forgotten someone.

- If you will be entertaining outdoors, spend time in the outdoor environment. Contemplate seating and food and drink service. Consider how to provide shade by day and what to do should it rain.

- Invitations—purchase and write invitations, or have them designed and printed. As a general rule of thumb, send invitations if hosting a party for 20 or more guests. For fewer guests, a phone call is a more personal touch.

- When printing or writing invitations, give guests an idea on how to dress. "Smart Casual" and "Dressy Casual" are now acceptable ways to describe desired attire. Old standards such as "Casual Attire" and "Coat and tie" are perfectly fine but may need more details for first time guests.

- Make sure invitations state a request that the guest respond. "Regrets Only" is more readily used but the French request, RSVP (Respond, if you please), is not only better etiquette but more helpful to the hostess who needs to know how many guests she will be serving.

(Note: Be a great guest, call your hostess either way and let her know how much you appreciate the invitation.)

Two Weeks Before the Party

- Make grocery list.
- Plan a cooking timeline.

- Prepare an "Other Jobs" list.
- Cook dishes that will freeze.

One Week Before the Party

- If the party is very important do trial run-throughs. Set up tables, check traffic patterns, test sound systems.
- With your RSVPs in hand, make final arrangements with caterers, bakers, liquor stores, furniture rentals, florists, bartenders, waiters, and babysitters. Confirm with them your address, directions to your home, delivery times/set up, and departure times/take down.

- Make seating arrangements and prepare place cards and/or menu cards if desired.
- Reconfirm expectations, arrival times, and payments with friends, family, and neighborhood kids who are helping out.
- If pests may be a problem when entertaining outdoors, spray yard, food set-up areas, and anywhere guests may mingle.
- Wash table linens and polish silver.

Three Days Before the Party

- Confirm number of guests and party equipment.

- Check your china and cutlery. Wash china and glasses.

One Day Before the Party

- Review cooking schedule again.
- Review "Other Jobs" checklist.
- Set table.

- Purchase food for last-minute preparation.
- Prepare vegetables and/or salads.

Party Morning

- Make list of jobs for the hired help.
- Buy fresh bread.

- Arrange flowers.
- Begin preparing the hot food.

One Hour Before

- Review all checklists.
- Try to relax.

- Complete hot food in oven.
- Set out appetizers that are not temperature sensitive.

Out of Thyme? Last Minute Touches

- Turn on background music.
- Adjust lighting to set the mood and light candles.
- Check powder room for paper supplies, soaps, and fresh hand towels.

- Freshen air with quick spritz of potpourri spray.
- Go through final instructions with any help staff.
- Remind yourself that you have planned well and should enjoy the event.

Thyme Management

Thyming is everything when preparing a meal. Coordinating the various components of the meal so that all items are ready to serve at one time is challenging. For example, the main course is typically the most difficult recipe on the menu to prepare. If the entrée is time consuming or grilled, select sides and salads that can be prepared ahead. If the entrée can be made in advance, you can choose sides and vegetables that require last minute attention. For less stressful and more successful meal preparation, use these suggestions as a guideline.

1) Prepare

Make a list of all items on your menu, noting preparation times. Include any garnishes to be used as well. Star items that can be done ahead and prepare those first:

- Wash salad greens and place between damp paper towels in the refrigerator.

- Make homemade salads dressings, garnishes, sauces, casseroles, etc.

- Slice butter pats and arrange on appropriate dish and chill.

- Prepare dessert and set aside.

2) Cook

Write out a cooking time schedule—Use the item that requires the longest cooking time as a reference point and schedule remaining items accordingly.

3) Serve

- Arrange salads on plates and place on table.

- Transfer prepared garnishes to table.

- Place ice in glasses and pour table beverages.

- Transfer hot items to serving dishes or begin food placement on dinner plates and serve.

Index

A

Index

$\mathcal{N}$

$\mathcal{O}$

$\mathcal{P}$

Thyme to Entertain

Please send me _____ copies   @ $20.95 each   _____
Kentucky residents add 6% sales tax   @ $ 1.25 each   _____
Shipping   @ $ 3.50 each   _____
Each additional book to same address   @ $ 1.50 each   _____
Gift wrapping   @ $ 1.25 each   _____

TOTAL ENCLOSED _____

Name _____

Address _____

City _____ State _____ Zip_____

Telephone (_____) _____

☐ Check or money order enclosed. Make check payable to Charity League.

☐ VISA/MasterCard Account #_____ Exp. Date _____

Signature _____

Mail to: *Thyme to Entertain*
c/o Charity League, Inc. • P.O. Box 7123 • Paducah, Kentucky 42001
or Fax order form to: (270) 442-2925

Thyme to Entertain

Please send me _____ copies   @ $20.95 each   _____
Kentucky residents add 6% sales tax   @ $ 1.25 each   _____
Shipping   @ $ 3.50 each   _____
Each additional book to same address   @ $ 1.50 each   _____
Gift wrapping   @ $ 1.25 each   _____

TOTAL ENCLOSED _____

Name _____

Address _____

City _____ State _____ Zip_____

Telephone (_____) _____

☐ Check or money order enclosed. Make check payable to Charity League.

☐ VISA/MasterCard Account #_____ Exp. Date _____

Signature _____

Mail to: *Thyme to Entertain*
c/o Charity League, Inc. • P.O. Box 7123 • Paducah, Kentucky 42001
or Fax order form to: (270) 442-2925